CW01652698

7

In this section

- The Assyrian conquest of Israel
- God's intervention in Hezekiah's life
- Isaiah's messages of hope and victory
- Josiah's programme of reform
- The pleas of Jeremiah for repentance

DAY **183** Hezekiah's reforms

A festival song
Psalm 81:1–16

Idols destroyed
2 Chronicles 31:1, 2 Kings 18:4

Hezekiah's further reforms
2 Chronicles 31:2–21

Israel's leaders denounced
Micah 3:1–12

Hoshea taken prisoner
2 Kings 17:3–4

Israel's wickedness
Hosea 7:1–2

Conspiracy in the palace
Hosea 7:3–7

Israel and the nations
Hosea 7:8–16

2 Chronicles 31:1–4

**1When all this had ended, the
Israelites who were there went out
to the towns of Judah, smashed
the sacred stones and cut down
the Asherah poles. They destroyed
the high places and the altars
throughout Judah and Benjamin
and in Ephraim and Manasseh.
After they had destroyed all of
them, the Israelites returned to
their own towns and to their
own property.
2Hezekiah assigned the priests
and Levites to divisions – each of
them according to their duties as
priests or Levites – to offer burnt
offerings and fellowship offerings,
to minister, to give thanks and to
sing praises at the gates of
the Lord's dwelling. 3The king
contributed from his own
possessions for the morning and
evening burnt offerings and for the
burnt offerings on the Sabbaths,
New Moons and appointed feasts
as written in the Law of the Lord.
4He ordered the people living in
Jerusalem to give the portion due
the priests and Levites so that
they could devote themselves to
the Law of the Lord ...**

For Thought and **Contemplation**

Following the celebration of the Passover, great spiritual reforms took place in Israel. This is how it ought always to be. The benefits we receive through prayer, Holy Communion and the ministry of the Word in the house of God on Sundays ought to be worked out in our own house on Mondays. And Tuesdays. And Wednesdays ...

"... continue to work out your salvation with fear and trembling, for it is God who works in you to will and to act according to his good purpose." (Phil. 2:12–13)

1300 BC | Ruth | 1200 BC | Gideon | 1100 BC | Samson

Assyrian Empire founded Deborah & Barak Samuel

Israel's punishment

DAY **184**

Hosea 13:1–6

When Ephraim spoke, men trembled;
he was exalted in Israel.
But he became guilty of Baal worship and died.
2 Now they sin more and more;
they make idols for themselves from their silver,
cleverly fashioned images,
all of them the work of craftsmen.
It is said of these people,
"They offer human sacrifice
and kiss the calf-idols."
3 Therefore they will be like the morning mist,
like the early dew that disappears,
like chaff swirling from a threshing floor,
like smoke escaping through a window.
4 "But I am the Lord your God,
[who brought you] out of Egypt.
You shall acknowledge no God but me,
no Saviour except me.
5 I cared for you in the desert,
in the land of burning heat.
6 When I fed them, they were satisfied ..."

The Lord condemns Israel
Hosea 8:1–14

Hosea's announcement
Hosea 9:1–9

The consequences of Israel's sin
Hosea 9:10–14

The Lord's judgment
Hosea 9:15–16

The prophet speaks
Hosea 9:17, 10:1–8

The Lord pronounces judgment
Hosea 10:9–15

God's love
Hosea 11:1–11

Israel and Judah are condemned
Hosea 11:12, 12:1–6

Further words of judgment
Hosea 12:7–14

Final judgment on Israel
Hosea 13:1–8

For Thought and **Contemplation**

It is important to remember that God's judgment of His people's sins is not merely retributive, but remedial. He isn't against us for our sin, but for us against our sin. Think about it. It's a thought worth holding in our minds throughout the whole of this day.

"But God demonstrates his own love for us in this: While we were still sinners, Christ died for us." (Rom. 5:8)

DAY **185**

Israel taken captive

Final judgment on Israel
Hosea 13:9–16

Hosea's plea
Hosea 14:1–3

Israel's restoration
Hosea 14:4–9

Samaria besieged
2 Kings 17:5, 18:9

Israel taken captive
2 Kings 17:6, 18:10–11

Reasons for Israel's downfall
2 Kings 17:7–23, 18:12

Prayer for Israel's restoration
Psalm 80:1–19

The Fall of Israel 721 BC

A vision of Babylon's fall
Isaiah 21:1–10

2 Kings 17:7–12

**[7]All this took place because the
Israelites had sinned against the
Lord their God, who had brought
them out of Egypt from under the
power of Pharaoh king of Egypt.
They worshipped other gods [8]and
followed the practices of the
nations the Lord had driven out
before them, as well as the
practices that the kings of Israel
had introduced. [9]The Israelites
secretly did things against the
Lord their God that were not right.
From watchtower to fortified city
they built themselves high places
in all their towns. [10]They set up
sacred stones and Asherah poles
on every high hill and under every
spreading tree. [11]At every high
place they burned incense, as the
nations whom the Lord had driven
out before them had done. They
did wicked things that provoked
the Lord to anger. [12]They wor-
shipped idols, though the Lord had
said, "You shall not do this." ...**

For Thought and **Contemplation**

One of the greatest mysteries of life is why God uses ungodly people or nations to chastise His own children. Surely one answer must be that if we fail to examine our own hearts, then God must do it for us. And the "examination board" He uses may not always be to our liking!

"My son, do not despise the Lord's discipline and do not resent his rebuke, because the Lord disciplines those he loves, as a father the son he delights in." (Prov. 3:11–12)

1300 BC | Ruth | 1200 BC | Gideon | 1100 BC | Samson

Assyrian Empire founded | Deborah & Barak | Samuel

The nations judged

DAY 186

Isaiah 14:28–32

28This oracle came in the year
King Ahaz died:
29Do not rejoice, all you Philistines,
that the rod that struck you is
broken;
from the root of that snake will
spring up a viper,
its fruit will be a darting,
venomous serpent.
30The poorest of the poor will find
pasture,
and the needy will lie down in
safety.
But your root I will destroy by
famine;
it will slay your survivors.
31Wail, O gate! Howl, O city!
Melt away, all you Philistines!
A cloud of smoke comes from
the north,
and there is not a straggler in
its ranks.
32What answer shall be given
to the envoys of that nation?
"The Lord has established Zion,
and in her his afflicted people will
find refuge."

A message about Edom
Isaiah 21:11–12

A message about Arabia
Isaiah 21:13–17

Judgment upon the Philistines
Isaiah 14:28–32

Judgment upon Moab
Isaiah 15:1–9

Moab's hopeless situation
Isaiah 16:1–14

Hezekiah defies Assyria
2 Kings 18:7–8

The Amalekites slain
1 Chronicles 4:39–43

Judgment against Ethiopia
Isaiah 18:1–7

Judgment against Egypt
Isaiah 19:1–15

Egypt will worship the Lord
Isaiah 19:16–25

For Thought and **Contemplation**

The theme of judgment, although very conspicuous in Old Testament times, is often missing from modern Christian thought. Yet make no mistake about it – judgment will come. As someone has said: "If God will not judge the nations for their sins, then He will surely have to apologise to Sodom and Gomorrah."

" ... the Lord ... comes to judge the earth. He will judge the world in righteousness and the peoples in his truth." (Psa. 96:13)

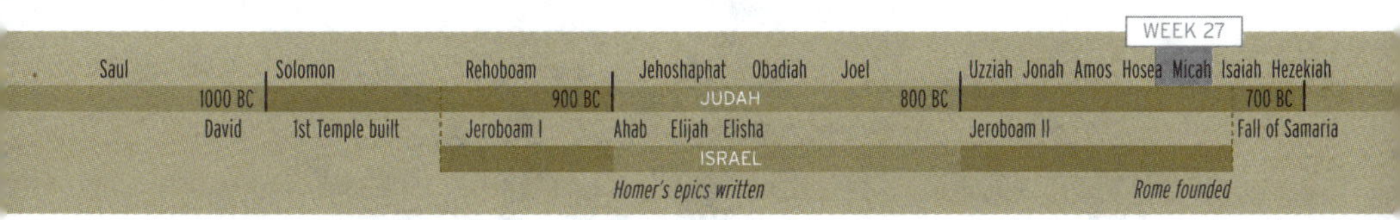

Assyria's coming destruction

The sign to Egypt and Ethiopia
Isaiah 20:1–6

Judgment against Tyre
Isaiah 23:1–18

Assyria, God's instrument
Isaiah 10:5–19

Remnant of Israel to be saved
Isaiah 10:20–23

Judgment against Assyria
Isaiah 10:24–27

The invader attacks
Isaiah 10:28–34

The peaceful kingdom
Isaiah 11:1–9

The exiles will return
Isaiah 11:10–16

Hymn of thanksgiving
Isaiah 12:1–6

Isaiah 10:28–34

28They enter Aiath;
they pass through Migron;
they store supplies at Michmash.
29They go over the pass, and say,
"We will camp overnight at Geba."
Ramah trembles;
Gibeah of Saul flees.
30Cry out, O Daughter of Gallim!
Listen, O Laishah!
Poor Anathoth!
31Madmenah is in flight;
the people of Gebim take cover.
32This day they will halt at Nob;
they will shake their fist
at the mount of the Daughter of Zion,
at the hill of Jerusalem.
33See, the Lord, the Lord Almighty,
will lop off the boughs with great power.
The lofty trees will be felled,
the tall ones will be brought low.
34He will cut down the forest thickets with an axe;
Lebanon will fall before the Mighty One.

For Thought and **Contemplation**

This point must never be forgotten: when God allows His people to fall into trouble, it is to humble them and bring their sin to remembrance. The ultimate end of all God's judgments, as they relate to His people, is the putting away of sin. He upsets us in order to set us up.

"The eyes of the arrogant man will be humbled and the pride of men brought low; the Lord alone will be exalted in that day." (Isa. 2:11)

1300 BC — Ruth — 1200 BC — Gideon — 1100 BC — Samson

Assyrian Empire founded — Deborah & Barak — Samuel

The Lord's judgments

DAY **188**

Isaiah 14:22–26

22"I will rise up against them,"
declares the Lord Almighty.
"I will cut off from Babylon her name and survivors,
her offspring and descendants,"
declares the Lord.
23"I will turn her into a place for owls
and into swampland;
I will sweep her with the broom of destruction,"
declares the Lord Almighty.
24The Lord Almighty has sworn,
"Surely, as I have planned, so it will be,
and as I have purposed, so it will stand.
25I will crush the Assyrian in my land;
on my mountains I will trample him down.
His yoke will be taken from my people,
and his burden removed from their shoulders."
26This is the plan determined for the whole world;
this is the hand stretched out over all nations. ...

Judgment upon Babylon
Isaiah 13:1–16

The return from exile
Isaiah 14:1–3

The king of Babylon's fall
Isaiah 14:4–11, 18–21

God will destroy Babylon
Isaiah 14:22–23

God will destroy the Assyrians
Isaiah 14:24–27

Judgment upon the world
Isaiah 24:1–23

A hymn of praise
Isaiah 25:1–5

God prepares a banquet
Isaiah 25:6–9

God will punish Moab
Isaiah 25:10–12

God's victorious people
Isaiah 26:1–11

For Thought and **Contemplation**

More and more judgment! When will God stop? The answer surely is – when men turn from their sin and follow the path of righteousness. And those who obey the divine command to cease from sin discover this encouraging truth – the Almighty is as great in mercy as He is in judgment. Hallelujah!

" ... unless you repent, you too will all perish." (Lk. 13:3)

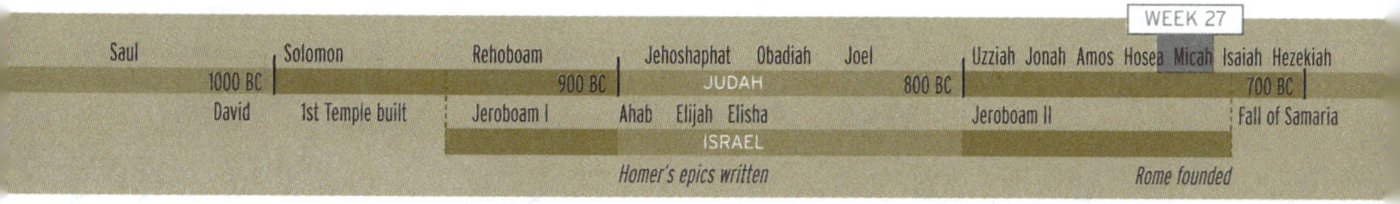

DAY **189**

The way of holiness

God's victorious people
Isaiah 26:12–19

Judgment and restoration
Isaiah 26:20–21, 27:1–13

The coming siege
Isaiah 22:1–14

God will punish His enemies
Isaiah 34:1–17

The coming victory
Isaiah 35:1–10

Hezekiah's divine healing
2 Kings 20:1–11

Hezekiah's pride
2 Chronicles 32:24–26

Isaiah 35:1–6

1 The desert and the parched land will be glad;
the wilderness will rejoice and blossom.
Like the crocus,
2 it will burst into bloom;
it will rejoice greatly and shout for joy.
The glory of Lebanon will be given to it,
the splendour of Carmel and Sharon;
they will see the glory of the Lord,
the splendour of our God.
3 Strengthen the feeble hands,
steady the knees that give way;
4 say to those with fearful hearts,
"Be strong, do not fear;
your God will come,
he will come with vengeance;
with divine retribution
he will come to save you."
5 Then will the eyes of the blind be opened
and the ears of the deaf unstopped.
6 Then will the lame leap like a deer,
and the mute tongue shout for joy ...

For Thought and **Contemplation**

Never let it be forgotten that God's way is a way of holiness. Did you know that the root meaning of "holiness" is "healthiness"? Perhaps this is a good moment to check your spiritual health. When we are unholy, we are unhealthy. How "healthy" are you at this present moment?

"Consecrate yourselves and be holy, because I am the Lord your God." (Lev. 20:7)

1300 BC | Ruth | 1200 BC | Gideon | 1100 BC | Samson

Assyrian Empire founded | Deborah & Barak | Samuel

The incomparable God

DAY **190**

Isaiah 40:12–15

12 Who has measured the waters in the hollow of his hand,
or with the breadth of his hand marked off the heavens?
Who has held the dust of the earth in a basket,
or weighed the mountains on the scales
and the hills in a balance?
13 Who has understood the mind of the Lord,
or instructed him as his counsellor?
14 Whom did the Lord consult to enlighten him,
and who taught him the right way?
Who was it that taught him knowledge
or showed him the path of understanding?
15 Surely the nations are like a drop in a bucket;
they are regarded as dust on the scales;
he weighs the islands as though they were fine dust ...

Hezekiah's illness and healing
Isaiah 38:1–8, 21–22

Hezekiah is thankful
Isaiah 38:9–20

Words of hope
Isaiah 40:1–9

God's care and protection
Isaiah 40:10–11

Israel's incomparable God
Isaiah 40:12–26

God reassures His people
Isaiah 40:27–31

God's promise to Israel
Isaiah 41:1–20

The Lord's challenge
Isaiah 41:21–29

For Thought and **Contemplation**

It's worth reflecting on the fact that our spiritual progress is largely determined by our view of God. If we hold in our hearts a limited or inadequate picture of Him, this will mirror itself in how we live, and what we ask of Him. Isaiah saw God as not just mighty but *almighty*. Do you?

"For by him all things were created: things in heaven and on earth, visible and invisible, whether thrones or powers or rulers or authorities; all things were created by him and for him." (Col. 1:16)

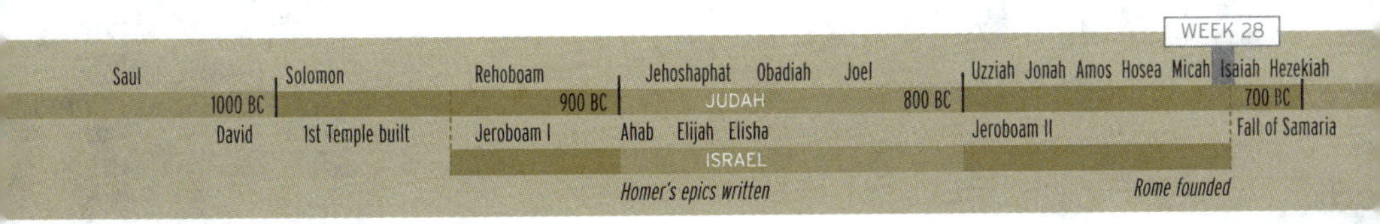

Israel: God's witness

- **The Lord's servant**
  Isaiah 42:1–9
- **A song of praise**
  Isaiah 42:10–13
- **God promises His help**
  Isaiah 42:14–17
- **Israel's failure to learn**
  Isaiah 42:18–25
- **God's promised rescue**
  Isaiah 43:1–7
- **Israel is God's witness**
  Isaiah 43:8–13
- **Escape from Babylon**
  Isaiah 43:14–21
- **Israel's sin**
  Isaiah 43:22–28
- **The only God**
  Isaiah 44:1–8
- **Idolatry ridiculed**
  Isaiah 44:9–20
- **The Creator and Saviour**
  Isaiah 44:21–28

Isaiah 43:8–12

8 Lead out those who have eyes but are blind,
who have ears but are deaf.
9 All the nations gather together
and the peoples assemble.
Which of them foretold this
and proclaimed to us the former things?
Let them bring in their witnesses to prove they were right,
so that others may hear and say, "It is true."
10 "You are my witnesses," declares the Lord,
"and my servant whom I have chosen,
so that you may know and believe me
and understand that I am he.
Before me no god was formed,
nor will there be one after me.
11 I, even I, am the Lord,
and apart from me there is no saviour.
12 I have revealed and saved and proclaimed –
I, and not some foreign god among you.
You are my witnesses," declares the Lord, "that I am God ..."

For Thought and **Contemplation**

Throughout time, God has always sought to maintain in His creation a witness to His honour and to His Name. In the Old Testament age, God's chief witness was Israel. In the New Testament age, His chief witness is the Church. Israel failed miserably. Do we?

"But you will receive power when the Holy Spirit comes on you; and you will be my witnesses in Jerusalem, and in all Judea and Samaria, and to the ends of the earth." (Acts 1:8)

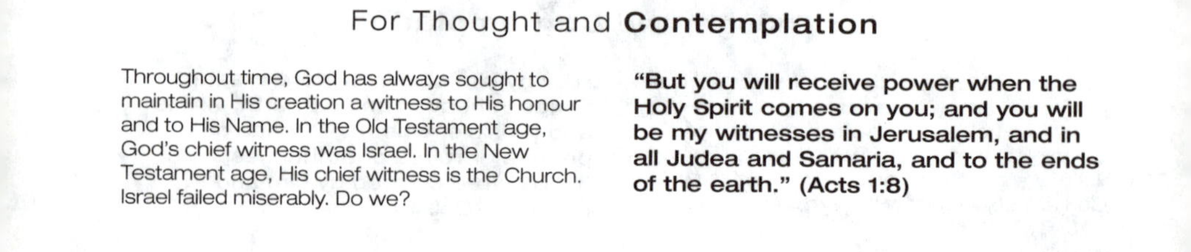

Prophecies Concerning
Gentile Nations in Isaiah

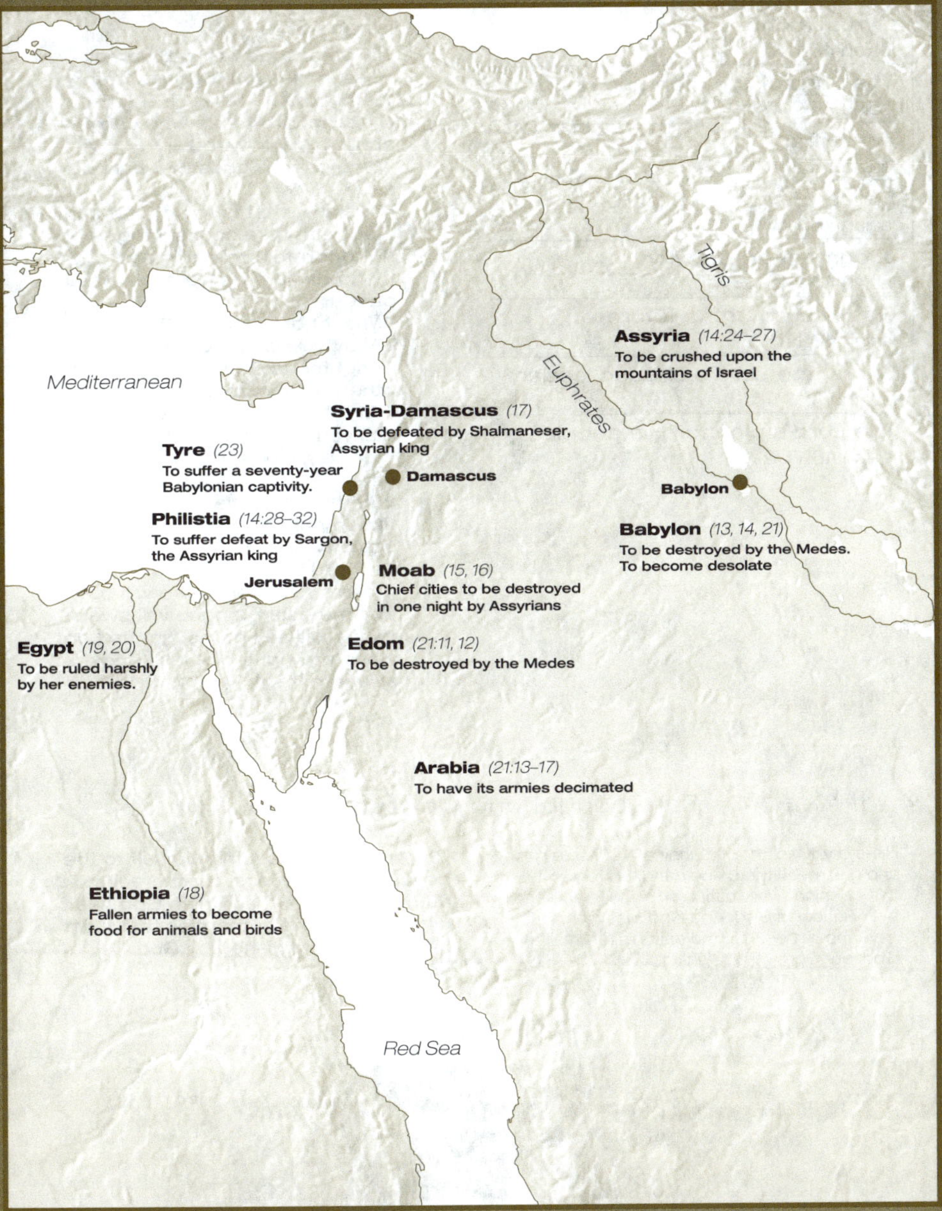

Lord of all

Isaiah 45:20–24

20"Gather together and come;
assemble, you fugitives from the nations.
Ignorant are those who carry about idols of wood,
who pray to gods that cannot save.
21Declare what is to be, present it –
let them take counsel together.
Who foretold this long ago,
who declared it from the distant past?
Was it not I, the Lord?
And there is no God apart from me,
a righteous God and a Saviour;
there is none but me.
22Turn to me and be saved,
all you ends of the earth;
for I am God, and there is no other.
23By myself I have sworn,
my mouth has uttered in all integrity
a word that will not be revoked:
Before me every knee will bow;
by me every tongue will swear.
24They will say of me, 'In the Lord alone are righteousness and strength.'" ...

For Thought and **Contemplation**

His-story. Men, though unaware of it, are girded and guided by the divine hand. So remember this – behind every nation is a leader, and behind every leader is God. And God, not men, will have the last word in the nation's affairs. It's God, our God, who *reigns!*

"Everyone must submit himself to the governing authorities, for there is no authority except that which God has established. The authorities that exist have been established by God." (Rom. 13:1)

1300 BC | Ruth | *Assyrian Empire founded* | Deborah & Barak | 1200 BC | Gideon | 1100 BC | Samson | Samuel

The restoration of Jerusalem

DAY **193**

Isaiah 49:8–11

8This is what the Lord says:
"In the time of my favour I will answer you,
and in the day of salvation I will help you;
I will keep you and will make you
to be a covenant for the people,
to restore the land
and to reassign its desolate inheritances,
9to say to the captives, 'Come out,'
and to those in darkness, 'Be free!'
They will feed beside the roads
and find pasture on every barren hill.
10They will neither hunger nor thirst,
nor will the desert heat or the sun beat upon them.
He who has compassion on them will guide them
and lead them beside springs of water.
11I will turn all my mountains into roads,
and my highways will be raised up. ..."

Israel, a light to the nations
Isaiah 49:1–7

Restoration of Jerusalem
Isaiah 49:8–26, 50:1–3

Obedience of the Lord's servant
Isaiah 50:4–11

The faithful encouraged
Isaiah 51:1–16

The end of Jerusalem's suffering
Isaiah 51:17–23

God will rescue Jerusalem
Isaiah 52:1–12

The suffering servant
Isaiah 52:13–15

For Thought and **Contemplation**

When God's people repent and confess their sins, the inevitable consequence is restoration and revival. Can you imagine what would happen if God's people throughout the world would seek His face in earnest confession and repentance? The restoration of Jerusalem would be as nothing compared to the glory and power that would flow through His Church.

"If my people, who are called by my name, will humble themselves and pray and seek my face and turn from their wicked ways, then will I hear from heaven and will forgive their sin and will heal their land." (2 Chron. 7:14)

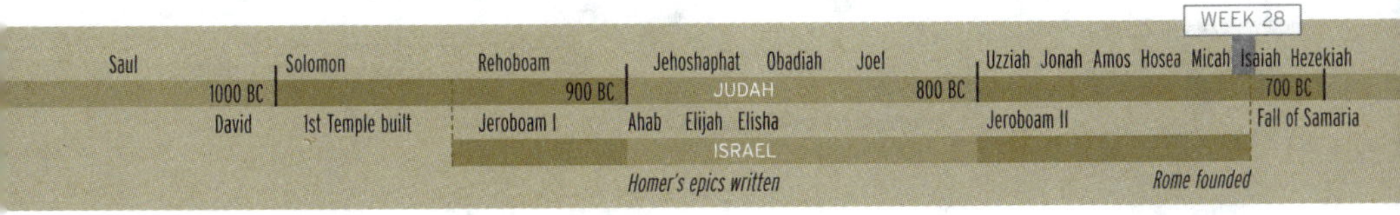

God's people comforted

- **Christ, the sinbearer**
  Isaiah 53:1–12
- **The Lord's never-ending love**
  Isaiah 54:1–10
- **The future Jerusalem**
  Isaiah 54:11–17
- **God's offer of mercy**
  Isaiah 55:1–13
- **God's worldwide invitation**
  Isaiah 56:1–8
- **Israel's leaders condemned**
  Isaiah 56:9–12
- **Israel's idolatry condemned**
  Isaiah 57:1–13
- **God's promise of help and healing**
  Isaiah 57:14–21

Isaiah 54:11–17

11"O afflicted city, lashed by storms and not comforted,
I will build you with stones of turquoise,
your foundations with sapphires.
12I will make your battlements of rubies,
your gates of sparkling jewels,
and all your walls of precious stones.
13All your sons will be taught by the Lord,
and great will be your children's peace.
14In righteousness you will be established:
Tyranny will be far from you;
you will have nothing to fear.
Terror will be far removed;
it will not come near you.
15If anyone does attack you, it will not be my doing;
whoever attacks you will surrender to you.
16See, it is I who created the blacksmith
who fans the coals into flame
and forges a weapon fit for its work.
And it is I who have created the destroyer to work havoc;
17no weapon forged against you will prevail ..."

For Thought and **Contemplation**

Let your thoughts linger today on Isaiah 53:5 – what someone has called the greatest verse of the Old Testament. It will only have meaning for you, however, if you have personalised it by faith. Can you say, "He was wounded for *my* transgressions ... bruised for *my* iniquities" (AV)? If you have not yet done so, receive the Lord Jesus Christ into your heart and life right now.

"For Christ died for sins once for all, the righteous for the unrighteous, to bring you to God. He was put to death in the body but made alive by the Spirit." (1 Pet. 3:18)

1300 BC | *Assyrian Empire founded* | Ruth | Deborah & Barak | 1200 BC | Gideon | 1100 BC | Samson | Samuel

Jerusalem's future greatness

DAY **195**

Isaiah 60:1–5

1 "Arise, shine, for your light has come,
and the glory of the Lord rises upon you.
2 See, darkness covers the earth
and thick darkness is over the peoples,
but the Lord rises upon you
and his glory appears over you.
3 Nations will come to your light,
and kings to the brightness of your dawn.
4 Lift up your eyes and look about you:
All assemble and come to you;
your sons come from afar,
and your daughters are carried on the arm.
5 Then you will look and be radiant,
your heart will throb and swell with joy;
the wealth on the seas will be brought to you,
to you the riches of the nations will come. ..."

True worship
Isaiah 58:1–12

Reward for keeping the Sabbath
Isaiah 58:13–14

The people's sins condemned
Isaiah 59:1–8

The people's confession
Isaiah 59:9–15

The coming of Christ
Isaiah 59:16–21

Jerusalem's future glory
Isaiah 60:1–5

All nations to honour God's people
Isaiah 60:6–9

God's favour and mercy
Isaiah 60:10–22

Good news of deliverance
Isaiah 61:1–11

For Thought and **Contemplation**

When God's people forsake their evil ways and turn back to Him, the future is bright indeed! That applies not only to the people of "natural" Jerusalem – the Jews – but also to those who belong to the "spiritual" Jerusalem – the Church. For all people, repentance before God is the key to everlasting joy.

"Repent, then, and turn to God, so that your sins may be wiped out, that times of refreshing may come from the Lord." (Acts 3:19)

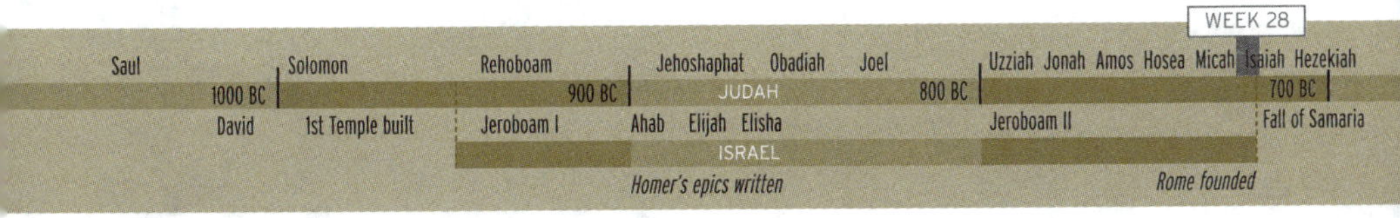

The Lord's mercy

God's care
Isaiah 62:1–5

The faithful watchmen
Isaiah 62:6–9

Announcement of salvation
Isaiah 62:10–12

Christ's victory
Isaiah 63:1–6

His mercy to Israel
Isaiah 63:7–14

Prayer of intercession
Isaiah 63:15–19, 64:1–5

A confession of sin
Isaiah 64:6–12

The calling of the Gentiles
Isaiah 65:1–7

Remnant preserved
Isaiah 65:8–10

Judgments on the wicked
Isaiah 65:11–16

The new Jerusalem
Isaiah 65:17–25

Isaiah 62:1–5

1 For Zion's sake I will not keep silent,
for Jerusalem's sake I will not remain quiet,
till her righteousness shines out like the dawn,
her salvation like a blazing torch.
2 The nations will see your righteousness,
and all kings your glory;
you will be called by a new name
that the mouth of the Lord will bestow.
3 You will be a crown of splendour in the Lord's hand,
a royal diadem in the hand of your God.
4 No longer will they call you Deserted,
or name your land Desolate.
But you will be called Hephzibah,
and your land Beulah;
for the Lord will take delight in you,
and your land will be married.
5 As a young man marries a maiden,
so will your sons marry you;
as a bridegroom rejoices over his bride,
so will your God rejoice over you.

For Thought and **Contemplation**

Here's a threefold truth that ought to stimulate your spiritual digestive system! Think about it every spare moment of this day: When the Messiah, the light of Jerusalem, comes (60:1) then righteousness will shine forth to the nations of the world (62:1) and Jerusalem shall be "a praise in the earth" (62:7).

"You are the light of the world. A city on a hill cannot be hidden." (Matt. 5:14)

1300 BC | Ruth | 1200 BC | Gideon | 1100 BC | Samson

Assyrian Empire founded | Deborah & Barak | Samuel

Micah's prophecies

Micah 4:9–13

9Why do you now cry aloud –
have you no king?
Has your counsellor perished,
that pain seizes you like that of
a woman in labour?
10Writhe in agony, O Daughter of Zion,
like a woman in labour,
for now you must leave the city
to camp in the open field.
You will go to Babylon;
there you will be rescued.
There the Lord will redeem you
out of the hand of your enemies.
11But now many nations
are gathered against you.
They say, "Let her be defiled,
let our eyes gloat over Zion!"
12But they do not know
the thoughts of the Lord;
they do not understand his plan,
he who gathers them like
sheaves to the threshing-floor.
13"Rise and thresh, O Daughter
of Zion,
for I will give you horns of iron;
I will give you hoofs of bronze
and you will break to pieces
many nations."
You will devote their ill-gotten
gains to the Lord,
their wealth to the Lord of all
the earth.

Vengeance is threatened
Isaiah 66:1–4

Jerusalem's future glory
Isaiah 66:5–14

Final ruin of the ungodly
Isaiah 66:15–24

A kingdom of peace
Micah 4:1–8

Final triumph of Israel
Micah 4:9–13

Christ's birth prophesied
Micah 5:1–6

Deliverance and punishment
Micah 5:7–15

God's controversy with Israel
Micah 6:1–5

The duties God requires
Micah 6:6–8

The wickedness of Israel
Micah 6:9–16

For Thought and **Contemplation**

The Old Testament prophets lived in eager anticipation of their coming Messiah. Do you? Someone has said: "The degree to which we desire Christ's coming is the degree to which we are experiencing His presence in our lives." The one is the natural outcome of the other.

"He who testifies to these things says, 'Yes, I am coming soon.' Amen. Come, Lord Jesus." (Rev. 22:20)

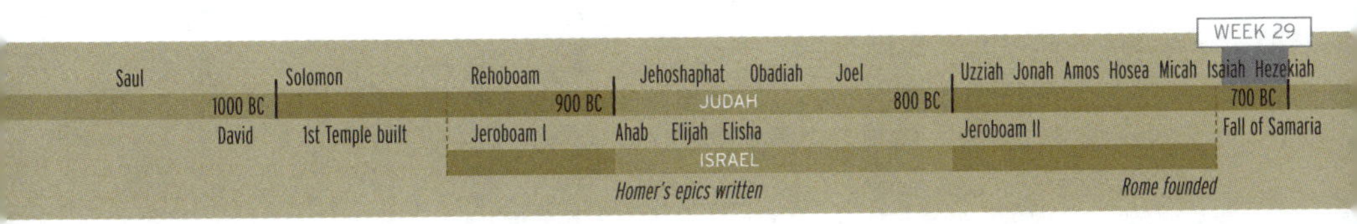

DAY **198** Jerusalem threatened

Israel's moral corruption
Micah 7:1–7

The Lord brings salvation
Micah 7:8–13

The Lord's compassion
Micah 7:14–20

Sennacherib and Hezekiah
2 Chronicles 32:1, Isaiah 36:1,
2 Kings 18:13–16

Jerusalem's defence prepared
2 Chronicles 32:2–8

Sennacherib threatens Jerusalem
2 Kings 18:17–26, 2 Chronicles 32:9–14,
Isaiah 36:2–11

Rabshakeh's defiance
2 Kings 18:27–35,
2 Chronicles 32:15–16, 18–19

Micah 7:8–12

8 Do not gloat over me, my enemy!
Though I have fallen, I will rise.
Though I sit in darkness,
the Lord will be my light.
9 Because I have sinned against him,
I will bear the Lord's wrath,
until he pleads my case
and establishes my right.
He will bring me out into the light;
I will see his righteousness.
10 Then my enemy will see it
and will be covered with shame,
she who said to me,
"Where is the Lord your God?"
My eyes will see her downfall;
even now she will be trampled underfoot
like mire in the streets.
11 The day for building your walls will come,
the day for extending your boundaries.
12 In that day people will come to you
from Assyria and the cities of Egypt ...

For Thought and **Contemplation**

The history of Israel is a series of ups and downs. One day repentant – the next day recalcitrant. Yet God loved them too much to let them get away with anything. Never forget that love is the reason for His discipline, not His discipline the reason for His love.

"Keep yourselves in God's love as you wait for the mercy of our Lord Jesus Christ to bring you to eternal life." (Jude v. 21)

1300 BC	Ruth	1200 BC	Gideon	1100 BC	Samson
	Assyrian Empire founded	Deborah & Barak			Samuel

Israel seeks help

DAY **199**

Isaiah 31:4–8

4This is what the Lord says to me:
"As a lion growls,
a great lion over his prey –
and though a whole band of shepherds
is called together against him,
he is not frightened by their shouts
or disturbed by their clamour –
so the Lord Almighty will come down
to do battle on Mount Zion and on its heights.
5Like birds hovering overhead,
the Lord Almighty will shield Jerusalem;
he will shield it and deliver it,
he will 'pass over' it and will rescue it."
6Return to him you have so greatly
revolted against, O Israelites. 7For
in that day every one of you will
reject the idols of silver and gold
your sinful hands have made.
8"Assyria will fall by a sword that is not of man;
a sword, not of mortals, will devour them.
They will flee before the sword
and their young men will be put to forced labour. ..."

Rabshakeh's defiance
Isaiah 36:12–20

Siege of Jerusalem prophesied
Isaiah 29:1–8

The Jews' hypocrisy
Isaiah 29:9–16

Future blessings
Isaiah 29:17–24

The Jews reproved
Isaiah 30:1–7

The disobedient people
Isaiah 30:8–17

God's mercies
Isaiah 30:18–26

Final ruin of the Assyrians
Isaiah 30:27–33

The folly of seeking help
Isaiah 31:1–3

God's care for Jerusalem
Isaiah 31:4–9

For Thought and **Contemplation**

The leaders of Judah were upset that Isaiah lectured them like children: "precept upon precept, line upon line ..." (Isa. 28:9–11, AV), and they completely ignored his warnings. Instead they had to listen to the stronger voice of their Assyrian conquerors. Beware of failing to heed the gentle reproofs of the Spirit, or else you may well be forced to heed the stronger voice of circumstances.

"You stiff-necked people, with uncircumcised hearts and ears! You are just like your fathers: You always resist the Holy Spirit!" (Acts 7:51)

WEEK 29

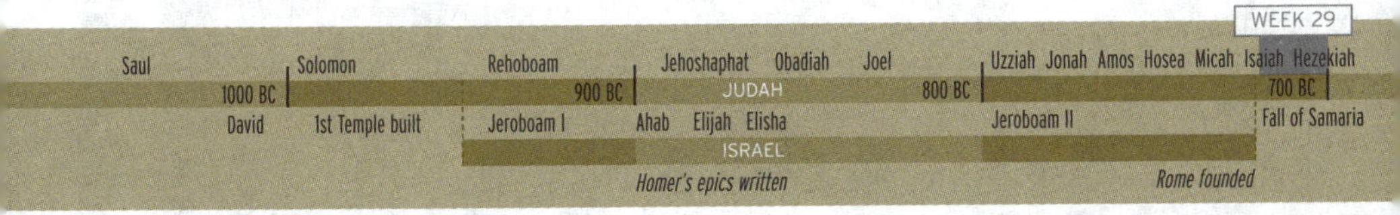

Seasons in Israel

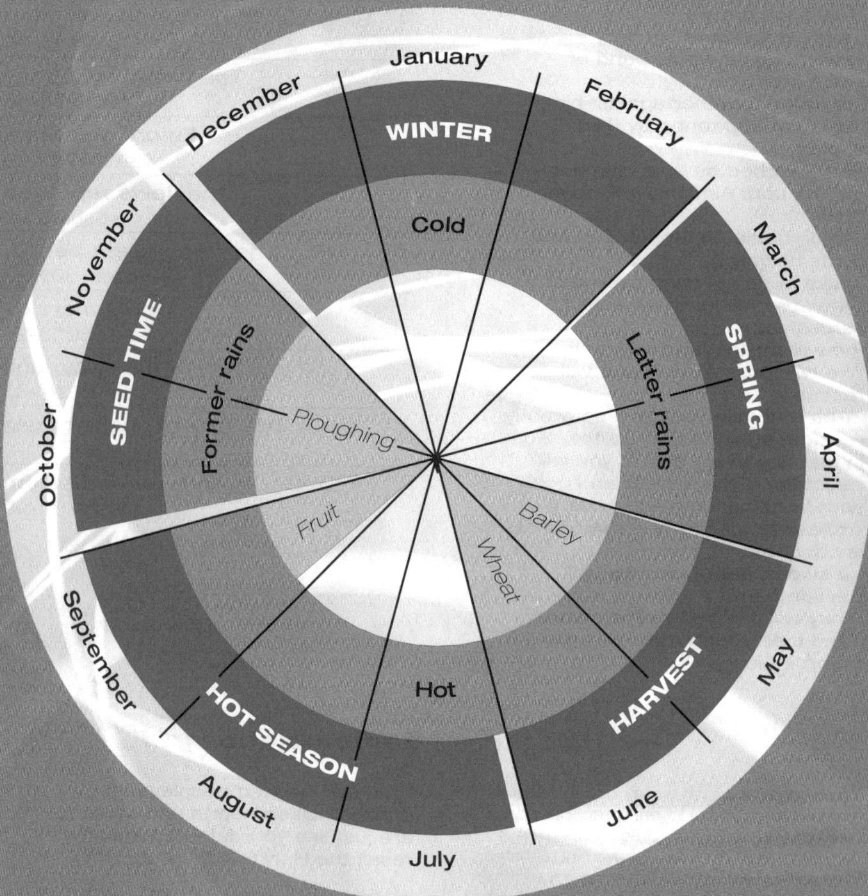

Hezekiah's consultation

DAY **200**

2 Kings 19:2–7

**2He [Hezekiah] sent Eliakim the
palace administrator, Shebna the
secretary and the leading priests,
all wearing sackcloth, to the
prophet Isaiah son of Amoz. 3They
told him, "This is what Hezekiah
says: This day is a day of distress
and rebuke and disgrace, as when
children come to the point of birth
and there is no strength to deliver
them. 4It may be that the Lord your
God will hear all the words of the
field commander, whom his mas-
ter, the king of Assyria, has sent to
ridicule the living God, and that he
will rebuke him for the words the
Lord your God has heard.
Therefore pray for the remnant
that still survives."
5When King Hezekiah's officials
came to Isaiah, 6Isaiah said to
them, "Tell your master, 'This is
what the Lord says: Do not be
afraid of what you have heard –
those words with which the
underlings of the king of Assyria
have blasphemed me. 7Listen! I
am going to put such a spirit in
him that when he hears a certain
report, he will return to his own
country, and there I will have him
cut down with the sword.'"**

Time of peace
Isaiah 32:1–8

Time of trouble
Isaiah 32:9–14

Time of blessing
Isaiah 32:15–20

A prayer for help
Isaiah 33:1–9

The Lord's warning
Isaiah 33:10–16

The glorious future
Isaiah 33:17–24

Hezekiah humbles himself
2 Kings 18:36–37, 19:1,
Isaiah 36:21–22, 37:1

Hezekiah consults Isaiah
2 Kings 19:2–7, Isaiah 37:2–7

A prayer for protection
Psalm 44:1–26

For Thought and **Contemplation**

How extremely comforting it must have been for Hezekiah when, concerned about the dishonour done to God by Rabshakeh's blasphemy, he was able to share his burden with the godly Isaiah. Do you have a prayer partner in whom you can confide? If not, ask God today to give you one.

"Then Daniel returned to his house and explained the matter to his friends Hananiah, Mishael and Azariah. He urged them to plead for mercy from the God of heaven concerning this mystery, so that he and his friends might not be executed with the rest of the wise men of Babylon." (Daniel 2:17–18)

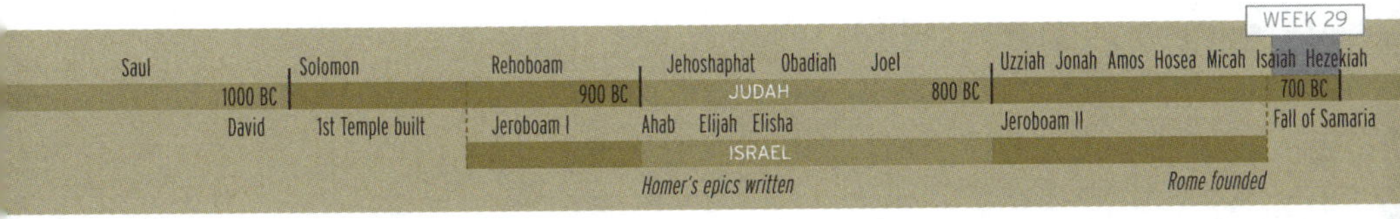

DAY **201** Hezekiah's prayer answered

Sennacherib's letters
2 Chronicles 32:17

He defies God
2 Kings 19:8–13, Isaiah 37:8–13

Hezekiah's prayer
2 Chronicles 32:20, 2 Kings 19:14–19, Isaiah 37:14–20

The psalmist's temptation
Psalm 73:1–14

How he gained victory
Psalm 73:15–20

How he profited by it
Psalm 73:21–28

Isaiah's response to Hezekiah
2 Kings 19:20–34, Isaiah 37:21–35

Isaiah 37:14–20

**14Hezekiah received the letter
from the messengers and read it.
Then he went up to the temple of
the Lord and spread it out before
the Lord. 15And Hezekiah prayed to
the Lord: 16"O Lord Almighty, God
of Israel, enthroned between the
cherubim, you alone are God over
all the kingdoms of the earth. You
have made heaven and earth.
17Give ear, O Lord, and hear; open
your eyes, O Lord, and see; listen
to all the words Sennacherib has
sent to insult the living God.
18It is true, O Lord, that the
Assyrian kings have laid waste all
these peoples and their lands.
19They have thrown their gods into
the fire and destroyed them, for
they were not gods but only wood
and stone, fashioned by human
hands. 20Now, O Lord our God,
deliver us from his hand, so that
all kingdoms on earth may know
that you alone, O Lord, are God."**

For Thought and **Contemplation**

Hezekiah's plea to God through Isaiah was not only heard, but answered. God not only listened but responded. Some think that prayer is merely talking to God. It's much more than that. Prayer is *conversation*; you talking to God and God talking to you. Is that the way it is in your prayer life?

"Come near to God and he will come near to you ..." (Jas. 4:8)

1300 BC | Ruth | 1200 BC | Gideon | 1100 BC | Samson

Assyrian Empire founded | Deborah & Barak | Samuel

Hezekiah's last days

Psalm 75:1–7

1 We give thanks to you, O God,
we give thanks, for your Name is near;
men tell of your wonderful deeds.
2 You say, "I choose the appointed time;
it is I who judge uprightly.
3 When the earth and all its people quake,
it is I who hold its pillars firm.
Selah
4 To the arrogant I say, 'Boast no more,'
and to the wicked, 'Do not lift up your horns.
5 Do not lift your horns against heaven;
do not speak with outstretched neck.'"
6 No-one from the east or the west
or from the desert can exalt a man.
7 But it is God who judges:
He brings one down, he exalts another.

Assyrian army destroyed
2 Kings 19:35–36, 2 Chronicles 32:21–22, Isaiah 37:36–37

God the Judge
Psalm 75:1–10

God the Victor
Psalm 76:1–12

Hezekiah's prosperity
2 Chronicles 32:23, 27–30, 2 Kings 20:20

The Babylonian ambassadors
2 Kings 20:12–19, Isaiah 39:1–8, 2 Chronicles 32:31

Hezekiah's death
2 Kings 20:21, 2 Chronicles 32:32–33

Assyrians settle in Samaria
2 Kings 17:24–41

For Thought and **Contemplation**

God extended Hezekiah's life by fifteen years but, regrettably, Hezekiah used those years for his own selfish endeavours rather than for God's glory. How sad when divine favour is prostituted and used for self-centred ends.

"When you ask, you do not receive, because you ask with wrong motives, that you may spend what you get on your pleasures." (Jas. 4:3)

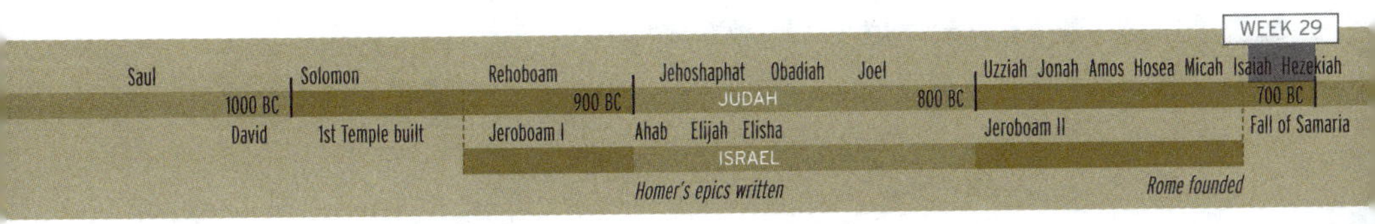

DAY **203** Manasseh turns to God

Manasseh's sinful ways
2 Kings 21:1–9, 2 Chronicles 33:1–9

God's displeasure
2 Kings 21:10–15, 2 Chronicles 33:10

Warning to Shebna
Isaiah 22:15–25

Sennacherib's death
2 Kings 19:37, Isaiah 37:38

Manasseh's sin and repentance
2 Kings 21:16, 2 Chronicles 33:11–13

His reforms
2 Chronicles 33:14–17

His death
2 Kings 21:17–18, 2 Chronicles 33:18–20

Amon's evil life and death
2 Kings 21:19–23, 26,
2 Chronicles 33:21–24,

Josiah becomes king
2 Kings 21:24, 2 Chronicles 33:25

2 Chronicles 33:11–15

**[11]So the Lord brought against them
the army commanders of the king
of Assyria, who took Manasseh
prisoner, put a hook in his nose,
bound him with bronze shackles
and took him to Babylon. [12]In his
distress he sought the favour of
the Lord his God and humbled
himself greatly before the God of
his fathers. [13]And when he prayed
to him, the Lord was moved by his
entreaty and listened to his plea;
so he brought him back to
Jerusalem and to his kingdom.
Then Manasseh knew that the
Lord is God.
[14]Afterwards he rebuilt the outer
wall of the City of David, west of
the Gihon spring in the valley, as
far as the entrance of the Fish
Gate and encircling the hill of
Ophel; he also made it much
higher. He stationed military
commanders in all the fortified
cities in Judah.
[15]He got rid of the foreign gods
and removed the image from the
temple of the Lord, as well as all
the altars he had built on the
temple hill and in Jerusalem; and
he threw them out of the city ...**

For Thought and **Contemplation**

Manasseh and Amon were two of the most evil men who ever lived. One wonders why God allowed such rulers to hold sway over His people. One thing, however, is sure – all will ultimately perish who refuse to walk in God's ways.

"Therefore the wicked will not stand in the judgment, nor sinners in the assembly of the righteous. For the Lord watches over the way of the righteous, but the way of the wicked will perish." (Psa. 1:5–6)

WEEK 30

700 BC | *Assyrians besiege Jerusalem* | Nahum Zephaniah Josiah Nebuchadnezzar | 600 BC | Daniel taken to Babylon | Jeremiah Habakkuk | FALL OF JUDAH | Jerusalem destroyed | Ezekiel | Exile in Babylon

The fall of Nineveh

Nahum 1:1–5

1 An oracle concerning Nineveh.
The book of the vision of Nahum
the Elkoshite.
2 The Lord is a jealous and
avenging God;
the Lord takes vengeance and
is filled with wrath.
The Lord takes vengeance on
his foes
and maintains his wrath against
his enemies.
3 The Lord is slow to anger and
great in power;
the Lord will not leave the guilty
unpunished.
His way is in the whirlwind and
the storm,
and clouds are the dust of his
feet.
4 He rebukes the sea and dries
it up;
he makes all the rivers run dry.
Bashan and Carmel wither
and the blossoms of Lebanon
fade.
5 The mountains quake before
him and the hills melt away.
The earth trembles at his
presence,
the world and all who live in it.

Josiah's godly character
2 Chronicles 34:1–2, 2 Kings 22:1–2, 23:25

God's justice and power
Nahum 1:1–8

The Assyrians overthrown
Nahum 1:9–15

Nineveh's destruction foretold
Nahum 2:1–10

The cause
Nahum 2:11–13

The fall of Nineveh
Nahum 3:1–19

Josiah's early reforms
2 Chronicles 34:3–7

Jeremiah's ministry begins 628 BC

Jeremiah's call and early vision
Jeremiah 1:1–19

For Thought and **Contemplation**

When a nation comes under the judgment of God then the mightiest defences are of no avail. It's a sobering thought that one day God will judge the nations of the world for their disobedience to His commands. And when He does, the most powerful nuclear defence strategy will be powerless to stand against His wrath.

"But they will have to give account to him who is ready to judge the living and the dead." (1 Pet. 4:5)

Zerubbabel and main party return — *Iron Age begins in Britain* — Ezra returns — Malachi

500 BC — 400 BC

Cyrus — Zechariah — Haggai — 2nd Temple built — Nehemiah rebuilds walls of Jerusalem

DAY **205** Jeremiah's first message

Jeremiah 2:4–8

4 Hear the word of the Lord,
O house of Jacob,
all you clans of the house of Israel.
5 This is what the Lord says:
"What fault did your fathers find in me,
that they strayed so far from me?
They followed worthless idols
and became worthless themselves.
6 They did not ask, 'Where is the Lord,
who brought us up out of Egypt
and led us through the barren wilderness, through a land of deserts and rifts,
a land of drought and darkness,
a land where no-one travels and no-one lives?'
7 I brought you into a fertile land
to eat its fruit and rich produce.
But you came and defiled my land
and made my inheritance detestable.
8 The priests did not ask,
'Where is the Lord?'
Those who deal with the law did not know me;
the leaders rebelled against me ...

For Thought and **Contemplation**

"I'll do it if I feel like it." Unfortunately many Christians adopt this attitude to God's commands. If Jeremiah had done that, then it would have changed a whole section of Old Testament history. Are you fighting the "God-said-it-but-I-don't-feel-like-it" battle? Then decide right now to do what God asks – *whether you feel like it or not.*

"If you love me, you will obey what I command." (Jn 14:15)

WEEK 30

700 BC — Assyrians besiege Jerusalem
Nahum Zephaniah Josiah Nebuchadnezzar
600 BC
Daniel taken to Babylon
Jeremiah Habakkuk
Jerusalem destroyed
FALL OF JUDAH
Ezekiel
Exile in Babylon

Prophecies of Jeremiah

1. **Fall of Jerusalem**
   (1:14–16, 4:5–9, 5:15–17, 6:1–6, 32:2–3, 38:17–18)
2. **Destruction of the Temple** (7:11–15, 26:6–9)
3. **Death of deposed King Jehoahaz in Egypt**
   (22:10–12)
4. **Unlamented death of King Jehoiakim** (36:27–30)
5. **Cutting of the royal line of King Jehoiachin**
   (22:24–30)
6. **Death of two false prophets and punishment of another - all three living in Babylon** (29:20–32)
7. **Death of a false Jerusalem prophet** (28:13–17)
8. **Capture and exile of a friend named Seraiah**
   (51:59)
9. **Failure of the Egyptian-Judean military alliance against Babylon** (37:5–10)
10. **Defeat of Egypt by Babylon at Carchemish**
    (46:1–12)
11. **Babylonian occupation of Egypt** (43:9–13)
12. **Seventy-year captivity of Judah in Babylon**
    (25:11, 29:10)
13. **Restoration to Jerusalem after the seventy years**
    (27:19–22; 30:3, 10–11, 18–21; 31:9, 12, 38–39; 33:3–9)
14. **Defeat of Babylon after the seventy years**
    (25:12, 27:7)
15. **Capture of Zedekiah** (21:3–7, 34:1–5, 37:17)
16. **Kindly treatment of the godly exiles in Babylon**
    (24:1–7)
17. **Final regathering of people of Israel**
    (30:3, 10; 31:8–12)
18. **Final rebuilding of the land of Israel**
    (30:18–21, 31:38–39, 33:7–9)

Josiah's godly reign

Further reproofs for sin
Zephaniah 3:1–7

God's mercy
Zephaniah 3:8–13

Restoration of Israel and Jerusalem
Zephaniah 3:14–20

Josiah repairs the temple
2 Kings 22:3–7, 2 Chronicles 34:8–13

The Book of the Law is found
2 Kings 22:8–10, 2 Chronicles 34:14–18

Josiah consults Huldah
2 Kings 22:11–20, 2 Chronicles 34:19–28

The king's covenant
2 Kings 23:1–3, 2 Chronicles 34:29–32

2 Chronicles 34:29–32

**29 Then the king called together
all the elders of Judah and
Jerusalem. 30 He went up to the
temple of the Lord with the men
of Judah, the people of Jerusalem,
the priests and the Levites – all
the people from the least to the
greatest. He read in their hearing
all the words of the Book of the
Covenant, which had been found
in the temple of the Lord. 31 The
king stood by his pillar and
renewed the covenant in the
presence of the Lord – to follow
the Lord and keep his commands,
regulations and decrees with all
his heart and all his soul, and to
obey the words of the covenant
written in this book.
32 Then he had everyone in
Jerusalem and Benjamin pledge
themselves to it; the people of
Jerusalem did this in accordance
with the covenant of God, the God
of their fathers.**

For Thought and **Contemplation**

Question: Why did some of Israel's kings turn out to be evil and wicked men while others were righteous? *Answer:* It depended not merely on their upbringing, their temperament or their view of life, but on their *willingness* to obey the word of the Lord. The will is a crucial issue in the battle between sin and evil. So ask yourself at this moment: How willing am I to obey the divine will?

"Whether it is favourable or unfavourable, we will obey the Lord our God, to whom we are sending you, so that it will go well with us, for we will obey the Lord our God." (Jer. 42:6)

a bird's eye view of **Zephaniah**

Place in the Bible

Thirty-sixth Old Testament book; fourteenth book of prophecy.

Special feature

The prominence of "The Day of the Lord"

Jeremiah's second message

Jeremiah 4:1–4

1"If you will return, O Israel,
return to me,"
declares the Lord.
"If you put your detestable idols
out of my sight
and no longer go astray,
2and if in a truthful, just and
righteous way
you swear, 'As surely as the
Lord lives,'
then the nations will be blessed
by him
and in him they will glory."
3This is what the Lord says to the
men of Judah and to Jerusalem:
"Break up your unploughed
ground
and do not sow among thorns.
4Circumcise yourselves to the
Lord,
circumcise your hearts,
you men of Judah and people
of Jerusalem,
or my wrath will break out and
burn like fire
because of the evil you have
done –
burn with no-one to quench it."

Israel better than Judah
Jeremiah 3:6–11

Pardon is promised
Jeremiah 3:12–20

Israel's repentance
Jeremiah 3:21–25

A call to repentance
Jeremiah 4:1–4

Judah is threatened
Jeremiah 4:5–12

Judah is surrounded
Jeremiah 4:13–18

Jeremiah's sorrow
Jeremiah 4:19–22

His vision
Jeremiah 4:23–31

Jerusalem's sin
Jeremiah 5:1–11

Israel's enemies
Jeremiah 5:12–19

God's warning
Jeremiah 5:20–31

For Thought and **Contemplation**

Many of God's people are spiritually shipwrecked because they believe that God will not be as strict as His Word suggests. Adam and Eve failed because of this. And, as our present reading shows, so did the people of Israel. Ask yourself right now: is this same attitude to be found in me?

"'Is not my word like fire,' declares the Lord, 'and like a hammer that breaks a rock in pieces?'" (Jeremiah 23:29)

Jesus and the Book

Jesus Christ often spoke about His second coming, which is closely linked in the Bible to Zephaniah's message of the Day of the Lord: see Matthew 24:42, "Therefore keep watch, because you do not know on what day your Lord will come."

Teaching

Zephaniah insists that the Day of the Lord, God's day of judgment, will come to Jerusalem. Like other prophets his message is that God must punish sin, especially idol worship, but for those who trust in God there will be mercy and rejoicing.

A Verse to Remember

"Seek the Lord, all you humble of the land, you who do what he commands. Seek righteousness, seek humility ..." (Zeph. 2:3)

The Passover is kept

The invasion of Jerusalem
Jeremiah 6:1–8

Rebellious Israel
Jeremiah 6:9–15

Israel's rejection of God's way
Jeremiah 6:16–21

Invasion from the north
Jeremiah 6:22–30

Josiah celebrates the Passover
2 Kings 23:21–23, 26–27,
2 Chronicles 35:1–19

Josiah's further reforms
2 Kings 23:4–14

2 Chronicles 35:1–6

**1Josiah celebrated the Passover
to the Lord in Jerusalem, and the
Passover lamb was slaughtered
on the fourteenth day of the first
month. 2He appointed the priests
to their duties and encouraged
them in the service of the Lord's
temple. 3He said to the Levites,
who instructed all Israel and who
had been consecrated to the Lord:
"Put the sacred ark in the temple
that Solomon son of David king of
Israel built. It is not to be carried
about on your shoulders. Now
serve the Lord your God and his
people Israel. 4Prepare yourselves
by families in your divisions,
according to the directions written
by David king of Israel and by his
son Solomon.**

**5"Stand in the holy place with
a group of Levites for each
sub-division of the families of your
fellow countrymen, the lay people.
6Slaughter the Passover lambs,
consecrate yourselves and
prepare [the lambs] for your fellow
countrymen, doing what the Lord
commanded through Moses."**

For Thought and **Contemplation**

Josiah's decision to celebrate the Passover – an ordinance that had been neglected in previous reigns – brought joy to God and delight to the people. The Almighty rewarded their commitment with evidences of His approval and favour. When we draw near to Him, He never fails to draw near to us.

"Let us draw near to God with a sincere heart in full assurance of faith, having our hearts sprinkled to cleanse us from a guilty conscience and having our bodies washed with pure water." (Heb. 10:22)

a bird's eye view of **Jeremiah**

Place in the Bible

Twenty-fourth Old Testament book; second book of prophecy.

Special Features

Autobiographical style.

Jeremiah's third message

Jeremiah 8:18–22

**18 O my Comforter in sorrow,
my heart is faint within me.
19 Listen to the cry of my people
from a land far away:
"Is the Lord not in Zion?
Is her King no longer there?"
"Why have they provoked me
to anger with their images,
with their worthless foreign
idols?"
20 "The harvest is past,
the summer has ended,
and we are not saved."
21 Since my people are crushed,
I am crushed;
I mourn, and horror grips me.
22 Is there no balm in Gilead?
Is there no physician there?
Why then is there no healing
for the wound of my people?**

Josiah's reforms
2 Kings 23:15–20, 2 Chronicles 34:33

Jeremiah preaches in the temple
Jeremiah 7:1–15

Birth of Ezekiel 622 BC

The people's disobedience
Jeremiah 7:16–29

Vengeance threatened
Jeremiah 7:30–34

Bones to remain unburied
Jeremiah 8:1–3

The people's stupidity
Jeremiah 8:4–13

The alarm of invasion
Jeremiah 8:14–17

Jeremiah's lamentation
Jeremiah 8:18–22

For Thought and **Contemplation**

Israel's greatest sin was that of idolatry – replacing the true object of worship with one which made lesser demands. But God will brook no rival in His universe, and therefore idolatry *must* be removed. If we don't get rid of the idols in our lives by our own volition, then we give God no other option than to topple them Himself.

"The acts of the sinful nature are obvious ... idolatry and witchcraft ..." (Gal. 5:19–20)

Jesus and the Book

Jeremiah looked towards the time when there would be a "new covenant" (Jer. 31:31–34), the covenant inaugurated by Jesus' death, which He spoke about at the Last Supper when He told His disciples: "This is my blood of the covenant ..." (Matt. 26:27–28).

Teaching

Jeremiah's prescription for Israel's sins of immorality and idolatry was to return to God in repentance. He insisted that this was much more important than relying on a foreign army to deliver them from the siege of Jerusalem.

A Verse to Remember

"This is the covenant that I will make with the house of Israel after that time," declares the Lord. "I will put my law in their minds and write it on their hearts. I will be their God, and they will be my people" (Jer. 31:33).

DAY **210** A further message

Jeremiah 10:12-16

12But God made the earth by his power;
he founded the world by his wisdom
and stretched out the heavens by his understanding.
13When he thunders, the waters in the heavens roar;
he makes clouds rise from the ends of the earth.
He sends lightning with the rain
and brings out the wind from his storehouses.
14Everyone is senseless and without knowledge;
every goldsmith is shamed by his idols.
His images are a fraud;
they have no breath in them.
15They are worthless, the objects of mockery;
when their judgment comes, they will perish.
16He who is the Portion of Jacob is not like these,
for he is the Maker of all things,
including Israel, the tribe of his inheritance –
the Lord Almighty is his name.

For Thought and **Contemplation**

How do you feel when you see God's hand of discipline on someone you know and love? Do you ignore it or do you "weep" over it as did Jeremiah? Pause for a moment to see if God wants you to intercede on behalf of an erring brother and sister. Let Jeremiah's deep concern be your example.

"Brothers, if someone is caught in a sin, you who are spiritual should restore him gently. But watch yourself, or you also may be tempted." (Gal. 6:1)

WEEK 31

700 BC
Assyrians besiege Jerusalem
Nahum Zephaniah Josiah Nebuchadnezzar
600 BC
Daniel taken to Babylon
Jeremiah Habakkuk
Jerusalem destroyed
FALL OF JUDAH
Ezekiel
Exile in Babylon

The sign of the ox yoke

Jeremiah 27:1–7

**1 Early in the reign of Zedekiah son
of Josiah king of Judah, this word
came to Jeremiah from the Lord:
2 This is what the Lord said to me:
"Make a yoke out of straps and
crossbars and put it on your neck.
3 Then send word to the kings of
Edom, Moab, Ammon, Tyre and
Sidon through the envoys who
have come to Jerusalem to
Zedekiah king of Judah. 4 Give
them a message for their masters
and say, 'This is what the Lord
Almighty, the God of Israel, says:
"Tell this to your masters: 5 With my
great power and outstretched arm
I made the earth and its people
and the animals that are on it, and
I give it to anyone I please. 6 Now I
will hand all your countries over to
my servant Nebuchadnezzar king
of Babylon; I will make even the
wild animals subject to him. 7 All
nations will serve him and his son
and his grandson until the time
for his land comes; then many
nations and great kings will
subjugate him. ..."**

Jeremiah's questions and God's answer
Jeremiah 12:1–6

The Lord's sorrow
Jeremiah 12:7–13

Babylon: the world power 612–539 BC

His promise
Jeremiah 12:14–17

Josiah slain
2 Kings 23:28–30, 2 Chronicles 35:20–24

Lamentation for Josiah
2 Chronicles 35:25–27

Jehoahaz' evil life
2 Kings 23:31–32, 2 Chronicles 36:1–2

Judah pays tribute
2 Kings 23:33, 2 Chronicles 36:3

Jehoahaz' death
2 Kings 23:34, Jeremiah 22:10–12

Jehoiakim made king
2 Kings 23:36–37 & 35, 2 Chronicles 36:5

The sign of the yoke
Jeremiah 27:1–11

Jeremiah in the temple court
Jeremiah 26:1–7

For Thought and **Contemplation**

Jeremiah's sign of the ox alerted the people to the fact that soon they would become subservient to the king of Babylon. He urges them to submit with meekness to this hard and humbling turn of providence in the sure knowledge that, in the lives of His people, God only allows what He can use.

"And we know that in all things God works for the good of those who love him, who have been called according to his purpose." (Rom. 8:28)

Zerubbabel and main party return
500 BC
Iron Age begins in Britain
Ezra returns
Malachi
400 BC
Cyrus
Zechariah Haggai
2nd Temple built
Nehemiah rebuilds walls of Jerusalem

Habakkuk's message

Jeremiah proclaimed a traitor
Jeremiah 26:8–19

Habakkuk complains of injustice
Habakkuk 1:1–4

The Lord's reply
Habakkuk 1:5–11

Habakkuk's further complaint
Habakkuk 1:12–17

Habakkuk must wait
Habakkuk 2:1–4

Judgments on the unrighteous
Habakkuk 2:5–20

Habakkuk's plea
Habakkuk 3:1–2

His prayer and praise
Habakkuk 3:3–19

Habakkuk 2:1–4

I will stand at my watch
and station myself on the ramparts;
I will look to see what he will say to me,
and what answer I am to give to this complaint.
2Then the Lord replied:
"Write down the revelation
and make it plain on tablets
so that a herald may run with it.
3For the revelation awaits an appointed time;
it speaks of the end
and will not prove false.
Though it linger, wait for it;
it will certainly come and will not delay.
4See, he is puffed up;
his desires are not upright -
but the righteous will live by his faith - ..."

For Thought and **Contemplation**

Almost all of the Old Testament prophets confessed to being confused by the ways and designs of God. But as they waited before Him, the confusion gave way to confidence. The secret of understanding God's ways is to "wait". Finally, the answer always comes.

"'For my thoughts are not your thoughts, neither are your ways my ways,' declares the Lord. 'As the heavens are higher than the earth, so are my ways higher than your ways and my thoughts than your thoughts.'" (Isa. 55:8–9)

a bird's eye view of **Habakkuk**

Place in the Bible

Thirty-fifth Old Testament book; thirteenth book of prophecy.

Special Features

Two rounds of questions and answers.

The first deportation

DAY **213**

Jeremiah 36:1–7

**1In the fourth year of Jehoiakim
son of Josiah king of Judah, this
word came to Jeremiah from the
Lord: 2"Take a scroll and write on it
all the words I have spoken to you
concerning Israel, Judah and all
the other nations from the time I
began speaking to you in the reign
of Josiah till now. 3Perhaps when
the people of Judah hear about
every disaster I plan to inflict on
them, each of them will turn from
his wicked way; then I will forgive
their wickedness and their sin."
4So Jeremiah called Baruch son
of Neriah, and while Jeremiah
dictated all the words the Lord
had spoken to him, Baruch wrote
them on the scroll. 5Then Jeremiah
told Baruch, "I am restricted; I
cannot go to the Lord's temple.
6So you go to the house of the
Lord on a day of fasting and read
to the people from the scroll the
words of the Lord that you wrote
as I dictated. Read them to all the
people of Judah who come in from
their towns. 7Perhaps they will
bring their petition before the
Lord, and each will turn from
his wicked ways ..."**

Obedience of the Recabites
Jeremiah 35:1–11

The Jews' disobedience
Jeremiah 35:12–19

Jerusalem's 20-year siege begins 606 BC

The wine cup of wrath
Jeremiah 25:15–38

Nebuchadnezzar besieges Jerusalem
Daniel 1:1

Some Israelites deported
Daniel 1:2–3

Prophecy concerning Israel's captivity
Jeremiah 25:1–11

Prophecies to be written
Jeremiah 36:1–8

God's promise to Baruch
Jeremiah 45:1–5

For Thought and **Contemplation**

Why would God allow His people to be deported and sent into exile? There could be only one reason: if they would not heed God's tender disciplines as given through the word of His prophets, then they must submit to His terrible disciplines as brought about through difficult circumstances. Got the point?

"These things happened to them as examples and were written down as warnings for us, on whom the fulfilment of the ages has come." (1 Cor. 10:11)

Jesus and the Book

Habakkuk states that God is his Saviour (3:18). The name "Jesus" means "The Lord saves". Jesus is the Saviour of the world: "... you are to give him the name Jesus, because he will save his people from their sins." (Matt. 1:21).

Teaching

Habakkuk observes unjust suffering, and God reveals that something even worse is in store for Judah – being crushed by the Babylonians. God shows Habakkuk that the only way a righteous person can survive is by being faithful to God.

A Verse to Remember

"I will rejoice ... in God my Saviour" (Hab. 3:18).

Section 7

Many of you are now experiencing the heat of summer when we really enjoy a cold refreshing drink. As you read God's Word allow it to refresh and encourage you. Reading through the Bible is not meant to be a business project but a life-refreshing and transforming experience. God gave His Word for our heart and spirit not just our intellect.

8

In this section

The Babylonian invasion of Judah
Exile in Babylon
Laments for Jerusalem
Daniel's rise to power
Ezekiel's prophecies of new life

Daniel tested

Egypt's defeat
Jeremiah 46:1–12

Nebuchadnezzar's conquests
2 Kings 24:7

Daniel, Hananiah, Mishael and Azariah
Daniel 1:4–7

Their refusal
Daniel 1:8–16

Their improvement in wisdom
Daniel 1:17–20

Uriah martyred
Jeremiah 26:20–24

Jeremiah's lament
Jeremiah 22:13–19

A fast proclaimed
Jeremiah 36:9

Nebuchadnezzar's dream
Daniel 2:1–13

The dream revealed to Daniel
Daniel 2:14–35

Daniel 1:17–20

17 To these four young men God gave knowledge and understanding of all kinds of literature and learning. And Daniel could understand visions and dreams of all kinds.
18 At the end of the time set by the king to bring them in, the chief official presented them to Nebuchadnezzar.
19 The king talked with them, and he found none equal to Daniel, Hananiah, Mishael and Azariah; so they entered the king's service.
20 In every matter of wisdom and understanding about which the king questioned them, he found them ten times better than all the magicians and enchanters in his whole kingdom.

For Thought and **Contemplation**

Daniel endured three great tests in Babylon: (1) the test of *food*, proving his obedience to God's law. (2) The test of the *dream*, proving his willingness to trust God's provision. (3) The test of the *lions' den*, proving his allegiance to God's Word. Could you have passed all three tests?

"These have come so that your faith – of greater worth than gold, which perishes even though refined by fire – may be proved genuine and may result in praise, glory and honour when Jesus Christ is revealed." (1 Pet. 1:7)

a bird's eye view of **Daniel**

Place in the Bible	Main Characters	Special Features
Twenty-seventh Old Testament book; fifth book of prophecy.	Daniel, Nebuchadnezzar.	Dreams and visions.

The sign of the linen girdle

Jeremiah 36:27–31

[27]**After the king burned the scroll**
containing the words that Baruch
had written at Jeremiah's dictation,
the word of the Lord came to
Jeremiah: [28]"Take another scroll
and write on it all the words that
were on the first scroll, which
Jehoiakim king of Judah burned
up. [29]Also tell Jehoiakim king of
Judah, 'This is what the Lord says:
You burned that scroll and said,
"Why did you write on it that the
king of Babylon would certainly
come and destroy this land and
cut off both men and animals from
it?" [30]Therefore, this is what the
Lord says about Jehoiakim king
of Judah: He will have no-one to
sit on the throne of David; his body
will be thrown out and exposed to
the heat by day and the frost by
night. [31]I will punish him and his
children and his attendants for
their wickedness; I will bring on
them and those living in Jerusalem
and the people of Judah every
disaster I pronounced against them,
because they have not listened.'"

Daniel's interpretation
Daniel 2:36–45

The king rewards Daniel
Daniel 2:46–49

The Word of God is read
Jeremiah 36:10–19

The king destroys the scroll
Jeremiah 36:20–26

Jeremiah replaces it
Jeremiah 36:27–32

The sign of the linen girdle
Jeremiah 13:1–11

The wine jar
Jeremiah 13:12–14

Jeremiah's warning
Jeremiah 13:15–27

The drought
Jeremiah 14:1–12

For Thought and **Contemplation**

Jeremiah's sign of the linen girdle was meant to show that Israel had corrupted themselves by their idolatry, so much that they were good for nothing. What an indictment! What sign, do you think, would Jeremiah give us if he were alive today, and wanted to indicate the true condition of the contemporary Christian Church?

"For it is time for judgment to begin with the family of God; and if it begins with us, what will the outcome be for those who do not obey the gospel of God?" (1 Pet. 4:17)

Jesus and the Book

Both Daniel and Jesus Christ prophesy of the end times. (See Mark chapter 13:26–27.)

Teaching

Daniel, a prisoner-of-war, shows his faith in God – as seen in the well known lions' den incident and in his interpreting dreams – and so taught his captors, and teaches us today, that true wisdom and ultimate power belong only to God.

A Verse to Remember

"Praise be to the name of God for ever and ever; wisdom and power are his. He changes times and seasons; he sets up kings and deposes them. He gives wisdom to the wise and knowledge to the discerning" (Dan. 2:20–22).

False prophets
Jeremiah 14:13–18

The people's plea
Jeremiah 14:19–22

The destruction of the wicked
Jeremiah 15:1–9

Jeremiah's complaint
Jeremiah 15:10–18

The Lord's reply
Jeremiah 15:19–21

The Lord's will for Jeremiah
Jeremiah 16:1–9

Return from exile prophesied
Jeremiah 16:10–15

The coming punishment
Jeremiah 16:16–18

Jeremiah's prayer
Jeremiah 16:19–21

The sin and punishment of Judah
Jeremiah 17:1–13

Jeremiah 16:19–21

19 O Lord, my strength and my fortress,
my refuge in time of distress,
to you the nations will come
from the ends of the earth
and say,
"Our fathers possessed nothing but false gods,
worthless idols that did them no good.
20 Do men make their own gods?
Yes, but they are not gods!"
21 "Therefore I will teach them –
this time I will teach them
my power and might.
Then they will know
that my name is the Lord."

For Thought and **Contemplation**

We are indebted to Jeremiah for reminding us that the heart of human problems is the problem of the heart (17:9). And what is the solution? This: "I the Lord search the heart" (17:10). Let God apply the searchlight of His Spirit today to those areas of your life where you have trouble trusting Him.

"Create in me a pure heart, O God, and renew a steadfast spirit within me." (Psa. 51:10)

WEEK 31

700 BC
Assyrians besiege Jerusalem
Nahum Zephaniah Josiah Nebuchadnezzar
600 BC
Daniel taken to Babylon
Jeremiah Habakkuk
Jerusalem destroyed
FALL OF JUDAH
Ezekiel
Exile in Babylon

Babylon

THE ASSYRIAN empire was replaced by the Babylonian. Nebuchadnezzar, its most famous king, conquered Judah in 597 BC, when Judah's king and skilled artisans were deported to Babylon. The city of Babylon was described by Herodotus as occupying about 200 square miles. It had eight ornamental gates, magnificent buildings and wide, tree-lined streets and double defensive walls. Its "hanging gardens", built by Nebuchadnezzar for his wife, were one of the wonders of the ancient world. The prophecy concerning Babylon in Isaiah 13 has been literally fulfilled. Its ruins are uninhabited except by wild animals. The region, once fertile, is now mostly barren marshland. There have been many excavations, and a few buildings have been reconstructed, but it has never been rebuilt.

Further signs

Jeremiah's prayer
Jeremiah 17:14–18

The Sabbath
Jeremiah 17:19–27

The sign of the potter's vessel
Jeremiah 18:1–10

The people's rejection
Jeremiah 18:11–17

A plot against Jeremiah
Jeremiah 18:18–23

The broken jar
Jeremiah 19:1–13

Jeremiah's conflict with Pashhur
Jeremiah 19:14–15, 20:1–6

His complaint
Jeremiah 20:7–18

Jehoiakim's rebellion
2 Kings 24:1

Message against Philistia
Jeremiah 47:1–7

Jeremiah 17:14–18

14 Heal me, O Lord, and I shall be healed;
save me and I shall be saved,
for you are the one I praise.
15 They keep saying to me,
"Where is the word of the Lord?
Let it now be fulfilled!"
16 I have not run away from being your shepherd;
you know I have not desired the day of despair.
What passes my lips is open before you.
17 Do not be a terror to me;
you are my refuge in the day of disaster.
18 Let my persecutors be put to shame,
but keep me from shame;
let them be terrified,
but keep me from terror.
Bring on them the day of disaster;
destroy them with double destruction.

For Thought and **Contemplation**

Do you feel a failure in your Christian life? A broken and defiled vessel? Then take note of what Jeremiah learned in the potter's house – namely, that God can refashion you into a new and glorious vessel. Ask Him to make you anew right now, and stay still under His touch as He puts you back on to the wheel of His purpose this very day.

"He restores my soul. He guides me in paths of righteousness for his name's sake." (Psa. 23:3)

WEEK 32

Nahum Zephaniah Josiah Nebuchadnezzar Jerusalem destroyed
700 BC | 600 BC | FALL OF JUDAH
Assyrians besiege Jerusalem Daniel taken to Babylon Ezekiel
Jeremiah Habakkuk Exile in Babylon

The Lord's judgments

Jeremiah 49:23–27

23Concerning Damascus:
"Hamath and Arpad are dismayed,
for they have heard bad news.
They are disheartened,
troubled like the restless sea.
24Damascus has become feeble,
she has turned to flee
and panic has gripped her;
anguish and pain have seized her,
pain like that of a woman in labour.
25Why has the city of renown not been abandoned,
the town in which I delight?
26Surely, her young men will fall in the streets;
all her soldiers will be silenced in that day,"
declares the Lord Almighty.
27"I will set fire to the walls of Damascus;
it will consume the fortresses of Ben-Hadad."

For Thought and **Contemplation**

Just as the New Testament shows how marvellous is God's mercy, so the Old Testament shows how terrible He is in judgment. Without judgment, grace would be sickly and sentimental, and without mercy, judgment would be terrifying and overwhelming. God needs to be seen in both aspects if He is really to be properly served and understood.

"It does not, therefore, depend on man's desire or effort, but on God's mercy." (Rom. 9:16)

Daniel — Zerubbabel and main party return — 500 BC — *Iron Age begins in Britain* — Ezra returns — Malachi — 400 BC

Belshazzar — 2nd Temple built — Zechariah — Haggai — Nehemiah rebuilds walls of Jerusalem

DAY **219** Second and third deportations: 598 BC

Jehoiakim's enemies
2 Kings 24:2–4

Second deportation: 3,023 captives
2 Chronicles 36:6–7, Jeremiah 52:28

Jehoiakim's death
2 Kings 24:5–6, 2 Chronicles 36:8

Jehoiachin
2 Kings 24:8–9, 2 Chronicles 36:9

His captivity foretold
Jeremiah 22:24–30

Third deportation: 10,000 captives
2 Kings 24:10–16,
2 Chronicles 36:10, Esther 2:6

Zedekiah
2 Kings 24:17–20, 2 Chronicles 36:11–16,
Jeremiah 37:1–2, 52:1–2

Israel's captivity foretold
Jeremiah 21:1–14

Jeremiah's message to the king
Jeremiah 22:1–9, 20–23

2 Chronicles 36:11–16

**11 Zedekiah was twenty-one years
old when he became king, and he
reigned in Jerusalem for eleven
years. 12 He did evil in the eyes
of the Lord his God and did not
humble himself before Jeremiah
the prophet, who spoke the word
of the Lord. 13 He also rebelled
against King Nebuchadnezzar,
who had made him take an oath
in God's name. He became stiff-
necked and hardened his heart
and would not turn to the Lord,
the God of Israel. 14 Furthermore, all
the leaders of the priests and the
people became more and more
unfaithful, following all the
detestable practices of the nations
and defiling the temple of the
Lord, which he had consecrated in
Jerusalem.**
**15 The Lord, the God of their
fathers, sent word to them
through his messengers again and
again, because he had pity on his
people and on his dwelling-place.
16 But they mocked God's messen-
gers, despised his words and
scoffed at his prophets until the
wrath of the Lord was aroused
against his people and there was
no remedy.**

For Thought and **Contemplation**

Ancient Israel is seen by many as being haughty in times of peace, fearful in time of trouble, downcast under the yoke of oppression, and unwilling to break with sin and idolatry until the last possible moment. Is this a description of many in today's Church? What do you think?

"See to it, brothers, that none of you has a sinful, unbelieving heart that turns away from the living God." (Heb. 3:12)

WEEK 32

Nahum Zephaniah Josiah Nebuchadnezzar Jerusalem destroyed
700 BC | 600 BC | FALL OF JUDAH
Assyrians besiege Jerusalem Daniel taken to Babylon Ezekiel
Jeremiah Habakkuk Exile in Babylon

Good and bad figs

DAY **220**

Jeremiah 23:5–8

[5]"The days are coming," declares the Lord,
"when I will raise up to David a righteous Branch,
a King who will reign wisely
and do what is just and right in the land.
[6]In his days Judah will be saved
and Israel will live in safety.
This is the name by which he will be called:
The Lord Our Righteousness.
[7]"So then, the days are coming," declares the Lord, "when people will no longer say, 'As surely as the Lord lives, who brought the Israelites up out of Egypt,' [8]but they will say, 'As surely as the Lord lives, who brought the descendants of Israel up out of the land of the north and out of all the countries where he had banished them.' Then they will live in their own land."

Faithless shepherds rebuked
Jeremiah 23:1–4

Israel's future restoration
Jeremiah 23:5–8

Message to prophets
Jeremiah 23:9–32

The Lord's burden
Jeremiah 23:33–40

Two baskets of figs
Jeremiah 24:1–10

Jeremiah's advice to Zedekiah
Jeremiah 27:12–22

Jeremiah's letter to the exiles
Jeremiah 29:1–14

Message to those who remained
Jeremiah 29:16–19

For Thought and **Contemplation**

Just as in Israel, so in today's Church there are "good and bad figs". The "good figs" are those who learn from corrective discipline, and the "bad figs" are those who continue in their wilfulness. In which basket do you think God might place you?

"Endure hardship as discipline; God is treating you as sons. For what son is not disciplined by his father?" (Heb. 12:7)

Zerubbabel and main party return | *Iron Age begins in Britain* | Ezra returns | Malachi

500 BC | 400 BC

Cyrus | Zechariah Haggai | 2nd Temple built | Nehemiah rebuilds walls of Jerusalem

Israel's bright future

Jeremiah's letter to the exiles
Jeremiah 29:20, 15, 21–23

Message to Shemaiah
Jeremiah 29:24–28

Shemaiah's punishment
Jeremiah 29:30–32

Coming trouble
Jeremiah 30:1–7

The Lord's promises
Jeremiah 30:8–17

Future restoration
Jeremiah 30:18–24

Israel's return home
Jeremiah 31:1–14

The Lord's mercy
Jeremiah 31:15–22

Future prosperity
Jeremiah 31:23–30

God's new covenant with Israel
Jeremiah 31:31–34

His everlasting mercy
Jeremiah 31:35–40

Jeremiah 31:31–34

31"The time is coming," declares
the Lord,
"when I will make a new covenant
with the house of Israel
and with the house of Judah.
32It will not be like the covenant
I made with their forefathers
when I took them by the hand
to lead them out of Egypt,
because they broke my covenant,
though I was a husband to them,"
declares the Lord.
33"This is the covenant that I will
make with the house of Israel
after that time," declares
the Lord.
"I will put my law in their minds
and write it on their hearts.
I will be their God,
and they will be my people.
34No longer will a man teach his
neighbour,
or a man his brother, saying,
'Know the Lord,'
because they will all know me,
from the least of them to the
greatest,"
declares the Lord.
"For I will forgive their wickedness
and will remember their sins
no more."

For Thought and **Contemplation**

It is characteristic of the Almighty that once His people are purified by oppression and exile, He acts at once to re-establish them and bring about their restoration. What would happen, do you think, if God's Church broke with all forms of idolatry, lukewarmness and indolence, and sought His face? There can only be one answer – *revival.*

"Restore to me the joy of your salvation and grant me a willing spirit, to sustain me. Then I will teach transgressors your ways, and sinners will turn back to you." (Psa. 51:12–13)

a bird's eye view of **Ezekiel**

Place in the Bible

Twenty-sixth Old Testament book; fourth book of prophecy.

Special Features

Visions are the characteristic feature of this book.

Ezekiel's vision

DAY **222**

Ezekiel 1:22–28

**22 Spread out above the heads
of the living creatures was what
looked like an expanse, sparkling
like ice, and awesome. 23 Under
the expanse their wings were
stretched out one towards the
other, and each had two wings
covering its body. 24 When the
creatures moved, I heard the
sound of their wings, like the roar
of rushing waters, like the voice of
the Almighty, like the tumult of an
army. When they stood still, they
lowered their wings.
25 Then there came a voice from
above the expanse over their
heads as they stood with lowered
wings. 26 Above the expanse over
their heads was what looked like
a throne of sapphire, and high
above on the throne was a figure
like that of a man. 27 I saw that from
what appeared to be his waist up
he looked like glowing metal, as
if full of fire, and that from there
down he looked like fire; and
brilliant light surrounded him. 28 Like
the appearance of a rainbow in
the clouds on a rainy day, so was
the radiance around him.
This was the appearance of the
likeness of the glory of the Lord. ...**

Hananiah's false prophecy
Jeremiah 28:1–16

His death
Jeremiah 28:17

Seraiah and Zedekiah visit Babylon
Jeremiah 51:59

Ezekiel's preparation
Ezekiel 1:1

His vision of God
Ezekiel 1:2–14

The four wheels
Ezekiel 1:15–21

God's throne
Ezekiel 1:22–28

Filled with the Spirit
Ezekiel 2:1–2

Ezekiel's commission as prophet
Ezekiel 2:3–10, 3:1–9

For Thought and **Contemplation**

Jeremiah prophesied to the remaining Jews in Jerusalem, while Ezekiel prophesied to the exiles in Babylon. Although God has one message, He uses many different messengers. If you run from the word of the Lord in your own church, then you will find the same message facing you in another. Worth pondering – don't you think?

"Where can I go from your Spirit? Where can I flee from your presence?" (Psa. 139:7)

Jesus and the Book

In chapter 34 Ezekiel contrasts faithful shepherds with uncaring shepherds, and in John 10:11 Jesus described himself as the "good shepherd" caring, leading and giving life to His followers.

Teaching

Through the six visions, six parables and ten signs Ezekiel comforted the downcast Jews, in exile in Babylon. He taught the Israelites how God had to punish sin, and also how God promised a new life through the activity of His Spirit.

A Verse to Remember

"I will give you a new heart and put a new spirit in you; I will remove from you your heart of stone and give you a heart of flesh. And I will put my Spirit in you ..." (Ezek. 36:26–27).

Ezekiel portrays the siege

Ezekiel appointed watchman
Ezekiel 3:10–21

God's glory
Ezekiel 3:22–23

Filled with the Spirit again
Ezekiel 3:24–27

The sign of the tile
Ezekiel 4:1–17

The sign of the sharp knife
Ezekiel 5:1–17

Idolatry condemned
Ezekiel 6:1–7

Remnant to be spared
Ezekiel 6:8–10

Desolation to come
Ezekiel 6:11–14

Ezekiel 3:24–27

24Then the Spirit came into me and raised me to my feet. He spoke to me and said: "Go, shut yourself inside your house. 25And you, son of man, they will tie with ropes; you will be bound so that you cannot go out among the people. 26I will make your tongue stick to the roof of your mouth so that you will be silent and unable to rebuke them, though they are a rebellious house. 27But when I speak to you, I will open your mouth and you shall say to them, 'This is what the Sovereign Lord says.' Whoever will listen let him listen, and whoever will refuse let him refuse; for they are a rebellious house.

For Thought and **Contemplation**

There are two essential prerequisites to an effective ministry for God. They are: (1) an overwhelming vision of God's power and greatness and (2) an understanding of where one fits into God's programme for the world. Ezekiel knew something of both these factors. Do you?

"Brothers, think of what you were when you were called. Not many of you were wise by human standards; not many were influential; not many were of noble birth. But God chose the foolish things of the world to shame the wise; God chose the weak things of the world to shame the strong." (1 Cor. 1:26–27)

Ezekiel's second vision

Ezekiel 8:1–6

**1In the sixth year, in the sixth
month on the fifth day, while I was
sitting in my house and the elders
of Judah were sitting before me,
the hand of the Sovereign Lord
came upon me there. 2I looked,
and I saw a figure like that of a
man. From what appeared to be
his waist down he was like fire,
and from there up his appearance
was as bright as glowing metal.
3He stretched out what looked like
a hand and took me by the hair of
my head. The Spirit lifted me up
between earth and heaven and in
visions of God he took me to
Jerusalem, to the entrance to the
north gate of the inner court,
where the idol that provokes to
jealousy stood. 4And there before
me was the glory of the God of
Israel, as in the vision I had seen
in the plain.
5Then he said to me, "Son of man,
look towards the north." So I
looked, and in the entrance north
of the gate of the altar I saw this
idol of jealousy.
6And he said to me, "Son of man,
do you see what they are doing –
the utterly detestable things the
house of Israel is doing here ..."**

The desolation of the land
Ezekiel 7:1–15

The distress of the few
Ezekiel 7:16–22

The captivity
Ezekiel 7:23–27

Idolatry in Jerusalem
Ezekiel 8:1–6

The hole in the wall
Ezekiel 8:7–12

Mourning for Tammuz
Ezekiel 8:13–14

The sun worshippers
Ezekiel 8:15–16

The Lord's response
Ezekiel 8:17–18

Marked men
Ezekiel 9:1–11

The Lord's departure
Ezekiel 10:1–15

For Thought and **Contemplation**

What foolishness was manifested by the elders of Israel in thinking that what they did in the dark could not be seen by the Lord. Someone has said that sin is the greatest of detectives. "Be sure your sin will find you out."

"Therefore judge nothing before the appointed time; wait till the Lord comes. He will bring to light what is hidden in darkness and will expose the motives of men's hearts. At that time each will receive his praise from God." (1 Cor. 4:5)

Zerubbabel and main party return | *Iron Age begins in Britain* | Ezra returns | Malachi

500 BC | 400 BC

Cyrus | Zechariah | Haggai | 2nd Temple built | Nehemiah rebuilds walls of Jerusalem

DAY **225** The Lord's condemnation

The Lord's departure
Ezekiel 10:16–22

Jerusalem is condemned
Ezekiel 11:1–13

God's promise to the exiles
Ezekiel 11:14–21

God's glory leaves Jerusalem
Ezekiel 11:22–25

Ezekiel the refugee
Ezekiel 12:1–7

The approaching captivity
Ezekiel 12:8–12, 15–16

The sign of the trembling prophet
Ezekiel 12:17–20

Objections answered
Ezekiel 12:21–28

False male prophets condemned
Ezekiel 13:1–16

False female prophets condemned
Ezekiel 13:17–23

Ezekiel 11:14–19

**14 The word of the Lord came to
me: 15 "Son of man, your brothers –
your brothers who are your blood-
relatives and the whole house of
Israel – are those of whom the
people of Jerusalem have said,
'They are far away from the Lord;
this land was given to us as our
possession.'
16 Therefore say: 'This is what the
Sovereign Lord says: Although
I sent them far away among the
nations and scattered them
among the countries, yet for a
little while I have been a sanctuary
for them in the countries where
they have gone.'
17 Therefore say: 'This is what the
Sovereign Lord says: I will gather
you from the nations and bring you
back from the countries where
you have been scattered, and I will
give you back the land of Israel
again.'
18 They will return to it and remove
all its vile images and detestable
idols. 19 I will give them an undivid-
ed heart and put a new spirit in
them; I will remove from them
their heart of stone and give them
a heart of flesh."**

For Thought and **Contemplation**

Much of Israel's downfall was due to the failure of her shepherds (i.e. leaders) – those who *plundered* rather than *protected* the flock. How true is the saying that it takes dedicated leaders to produce dedicated followers. Pray for your spiritual shepherd today.

"Obey your leaders and submit to their authority. They keep watch over you as men who must give an account. Obey them so that their work will be a joy, not a burden, for that would be of no advantage to you." (Heb. 13:17)

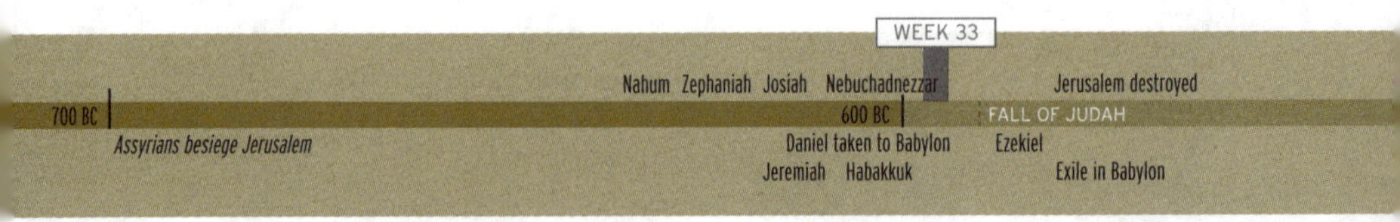

Jerusalem's adultery

Ezekiel 16:9–14

9 "'I bathed you with water and
washed the blood from you and
put ointments on you. 10 I clothed
you with an embroidered dress
and put leather sandals on you.
I dressed you in fine linen and
covered you with costly garments.
11 I adorned you with jewellery: I put
bracelets on your arms and a
necklace around your neck, 12 and
I put a ring on your nose, ear-rings
on your ears and a beautiful crown
on your head. 13 So you were
adorned with gold and silver; your
clothes were of fine linen and
costly fabric and embroidered
cloth. Your food was fine flour,
honey and olive oil. You became
very beautiful and rose to be a
queen. 14 And your fame spread
among the nations on account
of your beauty, because the
splendour I had given you made
your beauty perfect, declares
the Sovereign Lord.

Hypocrites threatened
Ezekiel 14:1–11

God's punishment
Ezekiel 14:12–23

Parable of the vine
Ezekiel 15:1–8

The Lord's covenant
Ezekiel 16:1–8

God's blessings
Ezekiel 16:9–14

Jerusalem's unfaithfulness
Ezekiel 16:15–22

Her adultery
Ezekiel 16:23–34

God's judgment on Jerusalem
Ezekiel 16:35–43

For Thought and **Contemplation**

Spend a few moments comparing the vine in Ezekiel with the vine in John 15. Remember that, in both cases, the only value of a vine is in the fruit it produces; its wood is quite useless (Ezek. 15:3). How much fruit is growing on your vine?

"I am the vine; you are the branches. If a man remains in me and I in him, he will bear much fruit; apart from me you can do nothing." (Jn. 15:5)

Zerubbabel and main party return
Iron Age begins in Britain
Ezra returns
Malachi
500 BC
400 BC
Cyrus
Zechariah Haggai
2nd Temple built
Nehemiah rebuilds walls of Jerusalem

DAY **227**

A parable explained

Ezekiel 18:30–32

**30"Therefore, O house of Israel,
I will judge you, each one
according to his ways, declares
the Sovereign Lord. Repent! Turn
away from all your offences; then
sin will not be your downfall. 31Rid
yourselves of all the offences you
have committed, and get a new
heart and a new spirit. Why will
you die, O house of Israel? 32For
I take no pleasure in the death
of anyone, declares the Sovereign
Lord. Repent and live!**

For Thought and **Contemplation**

There is only one word to describe the act of playing fast and loose with spiritual things – *prostitution.* It's a grim and horrifying word, but how else can God view the condition of those who pledge their fidelity to Him and then renege on their commitment?

"Now it is required that those who have been given a trust must prove faithful" (1 Cor. 4:2)

WEEK 33

700 BC | *Assyrians besiege Jerusalem*

Nahum Zephaniah Josiah Nebuchadnezzar

600 BC | Daniel taken to Babylon

Jeremiah Habakkuk

Jerusalem destroyed

FALL OF JUDAH

Ezekiel

Exile in Babylon

The Lord's reminder

DAY **228**

Ezekiel 20:27–31

27"Therefore, son of man, speak
to the people of Israel and say to
them, 'This is what the Sovereign
Lord says: In this also your fathers
blasphemed me by forsaking me:
28When I brought them into the
land I had sworn to give them and
they saw any high hill or any leafy
tree, there they offered their
sacrifices, made offerings that
provoked me to anger, presented
their fragrant incense and poured
out their drink offerings. 29Then
I said to them: What is this high
place you go to?'" (It is called
Bamah to this day.)
30"Therefore say to the house of
Israel: 'This is what the Sovereign
Lord says: Will you defile your-
selves the way your fathers did
and lust after their vile images?
31When you offer your gifts - the
sacrifice of your sons in the fire -
you continue to defile yourselves
with all your idols to this day. Am
I to let you enquire of me, O house
of Israel? As surely as I live,
declares the Sovereign Lord, I will
not let you enquire of me.' "

A lament for Israel's princes
Ezekiel 19:1-9

Another lament
Ezekiel 19:10–14

A reminder to the leaders
Ezekiel 20:1-9

In the wilderness
Ezekiel 20:10–26

In Canaan
Ezekiel 20:27–32

Pardon and restoration
Ezekiel 20:33–44

Prophecy against Jerusalem
Ezekiel 20:45–49

The Lord's sword
Ezekiel 21:1-7

For Thought and **Contemplation**

Why is it that we have to learn things the *hard* way? Israel had received so many warnings from God, yet they persisted in following their own stubborn and wilful ways. Know anyone else like that?

"We must pay more careful attention, therefore, to what we have heard, so that we do not drift away." (Heb. 2:1)

Zerubbabel and main party return | *Iron Age begins in Britain* | Ezra returns | Malachi

500 BC | 400 BC

Cyrus | Zechariah Haggai | 2nd Temple built | Nehemiah rebuilds walls of Jerusalem

DAY **229** God's refinery

Judgment by the sword
Ezekiel 21:8–17

The king of Babylon's approach
Ezekiel 21:18–27

The Ammonites' destruction
Ezekiel 21:28–32

The sins of Jerusalem
Ezekiel 22:1–16

God's furnace
Ezekiel 22:17–22

The sins of Israel's leaders
Ezekiel 22:23–31

The lustful sisters
Ezekiel 23:1–21

Ezekiel 22:17–22

**17Then the word of the Lord came
to me: 18"Son of man, the house of
Israel has become dross to me; all
of them are the copper, tin, iron
and lead left inside a furnace.
They are but the dross of silver.
19Therefore this is what the
Sovereign Lord says: 'Because
you have all become dross, I will
gather you into Jerusalem. 20As
men gather silver, copper, iron,
lead and tin into a furnace to melt
it with a fiery blast, so will I gather
you in my anger and my wrath and
put you inside the city and melt you.
21I will gather you and I will blow on
you with my fiery wrath, and you
will be melted inside her. 22As silver
is melted in a furnace, so you will
be melted inside her, and you will
know that I the Lord have poured
out my wrath upon you.'"**

For Thought and **Contemplation**

Israel spent much of their time in God's refinery. This was because, as we have seen, they failed to heed His Word. Ever been in God's refinery? Perhaps you are there right now. The heat is intense and the pressure is relentless, but the results are well worth the cost. You'll see.

"For you, O God, tested us; you refined us like silver." (Psa. 66:10)

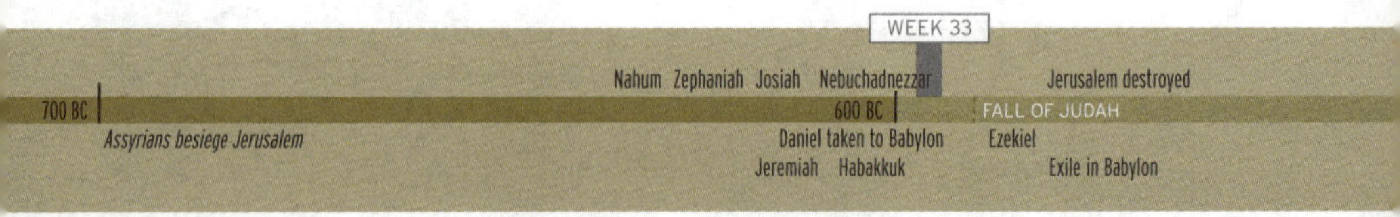

The Diaspora

The term "Diaspora" refers to Jews who live outside of Palestine (now Israel). Moses had warned the Israelites that they would be scattered among the Gentiles if they deserted the true God and worshipped idols. This scattering began through the Assyrian and Babylonian captivities, and became worldwide after the destruction of Jerusalem and the Temple in AD 70.

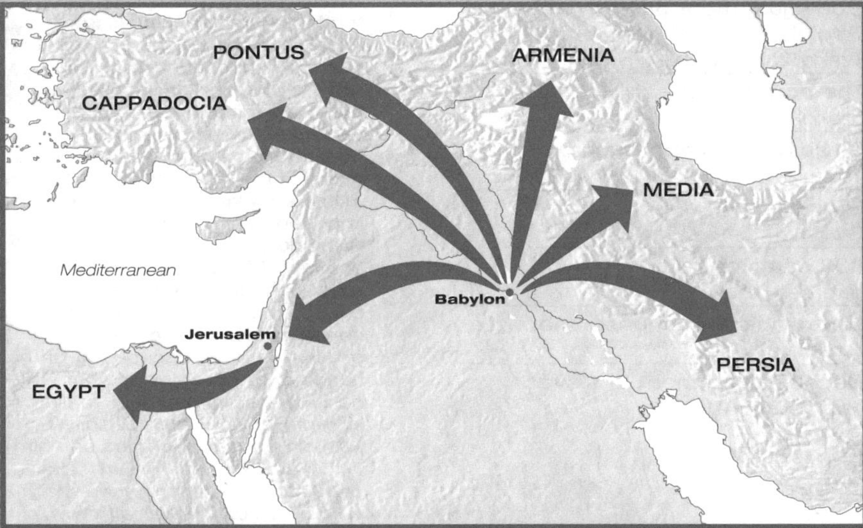

Famous sayings of Jeremiah

"Is there no balm in Gilead? Is there no physician there? Why then is there no healing for the wound of my people?" (8:22)

"Can the Ethiopian change his skin or the leopard its spots? Neither can you do good who are accustomed to doing evil." (13:23)

"The heart is deceitful above all things and beyond cure. Who can understand it?" (17:9)

"Is not my word like fire ... and like a hammer that breaks a rock in pieces?" (23:29)

"Call to me and I will answer you and tell you great and unsearchable things you do not know." (33:3)

DAY **230**

The fourth deportation: 588 BC

God's judgment on Oholibah
Ezekiel 23:22–35

God's judgment on Oholah and Oholibah
Ezekiel 23:36–49

The boiling cauldron
Ezekiel 24:1–14, 19–27

City's capture approaches
Jeremiah 52:3–5, 39:1, 2 Kings 25:1–2

Ezekiel's wife dies
Ezekiel 24:15–18

832 captives taken
Jeremiah 52:29

Jeremiah's first imprisonment
Jeremiah 32:1–5

Deceitful treatment of slaves
Jeremiah 34:8–11

Jeremiah 32:1–5

**[1]This is the word that came to
Jeremiah from the Lord in the
tenth year of Zedekiah king of
Judah, which was the eighteenth
year of Nebuchadnezzar. [2]The
army of the king of Babylon was
then besieging Jerusalem, and
Jeremiah the prophet was
confined in the courtyard of the
guard in the royal palace of Judah.
[3]Now Zedekiah king of Judah had
imprisoned him there, saying,
"Why do you prophesy as you do?
You say, 'This is what the Lord
says: I am about to hand this city
over to the king of Babylon, and
he will capture it. [4]Zedekiah king
of Judah will not escape out of the
hands of the Babylonians but will
certainly be handed over to the
king of Babylon, and will speak
with him face to face and see him
with his own eyes. [5]He will take
Zedekiah to Babylon, where he
will remain until I deal with him,
declares the Lord. If you fight
against the Babylonians, you
will not succeed.'"**

For Thought and **Contemplation**

By now the message that we either "take God's way or take the consequences" will undoubtedly have got home to you. Isolate one area of your life where you are going your own way, and draw up an alternative plan – God's plan. Then keep a diary of your progress and watch how things work out.

"In all your ways acknowledge him, and he will make your paths straight. Do not be wise in your own eyes; fear the Lord and shun evil." (Prov. 3:6–7)

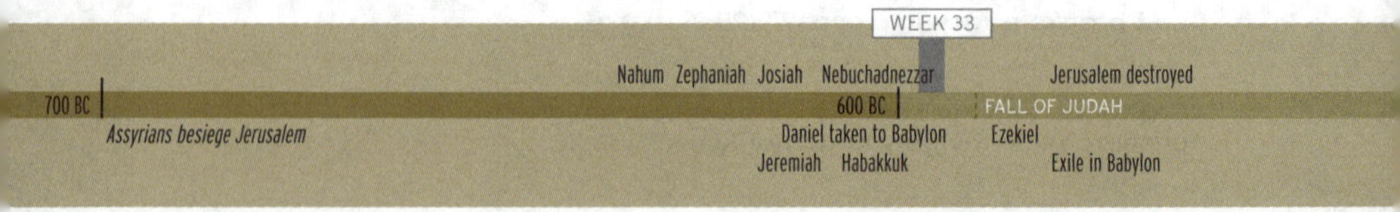

The overthrow of Tyre

DAY **231**

Ezekiel 26:7–14

**7"For this is what the Sovereign
Lord says: From the north I am
going to bring against Tyre
Nebuchadnezzar king of Babylon
... 9He will direct the blows of his
battering-rams against your walls
and demolish your towers with his
weapons. 10His horses will be so
many that they will cover you with
dust. Your walls will tremble at the
noise of the war horses, wagons
and chariots when he enters your
gates as men enter a city whose
walls have been broken through.
11The hoofs of his horses will trample
all your streets; he will kill your
people with the sword, and your
strong pillars will fall to the ground.
12They will plunder your wealth and
loot your merchandise; they will
break down your walls and demolish
your fine houses and throw your
stones, timber and rubble into the
sea. 13I will put an end to your
noisy songs, and the music of your
harps will be heard no more. 14I will
make you a bare rock, and you will
become a place to spread fish-
nets. You will never be rebuilt, for
I the Lord have spoken, declares
the Sovereign Lord.**

Dishonourable treatment punished
Jeremiah 34:12–22

Prophecy against Egypt
Ezekiel 29:1–7

The desolation of Egypt
Ezekiel 29:8–16

Tyre's rejoicing
Ezekiel 26:1–2

Tyre's enemy
Ezekiel 26:3–6

Tyre's attacker
Ezekiel 26:7–8

Tyre's destruction
Ezekiel 26:9–14

A terrifying example
Ezekiel 26:15–21

Tyre's funeral song
Ezekiel 27:1–25

For Thought and **Contemplation**

One of the greatest dangers we face in life is prosperity – whether it be financial, social or spiritual. It's the successful person who is in danger of forgetting their dependency on God. Self-sufficiency brought Tyre down to ruins. Watch that it doesn't do the same to you.

"So, if you think you are standing firm, be careful that you don't fall!" (1 Cor. 10:12)

Zerubbabel and main party return — 500 BC — *Iron Age begins in Britain* — Ezra returns — Malachi — 400 BC

Cyrus — Zechariah Haggai — 2nd Temple built — Nehemiah rebuilds walls of Jerusalem

DAY **232** Further prophecies

Tyre's funeral song
Ezekiel 27:26–36

The fall of the king of Tyre
Ezekiel 28:1–12, 19

Prophecy against Pharaoh
Ezekiel 30:20–26

Further prophecy against Egypt
Ezekiel 31:1–18

Jeremiah's advice sought
Jeremiah 37:3–4

Egyptian intervention
Jeremiah 37:5

Egyptian army to return home
Jeremiah 37:6–10

Jeremiah arrested, then released
Jeremiah 37:11–21

Jeremiah 37:6–10

**6 Then the word of the Lord came
to Jeremiah the prophet: 7 "This is
what the Lord, the God of Israel,
says: Tell the king of Judah, who
sent you to enquire of me,
'Pharaoh's army, which has
marched out to support you, will
go back to its own land, to Egypt.
8 Then the Babylonians will return
and attack this city; they will
capture it and burn it down.'
9 This is what the Lord says: Do
not deceive yourselves, thinking,
'The Babylonians will surely leave
us.' They will not! 10 Even if you
were to defeat the entire
Babylonian army that is attacking
you and only wounded men were
left in their tents, they would come
out and burn this city down."**

For Thought and **Contemplation**

Ever heard the statement: Cheer up, things could be worse. So you cheered up, and sure enough – things got worse! Jeremiah could have identified with that. How did he cope? By living above his circumstances rather than under them! Have you learned that secret yet?

"But he said to me, 'My grace is sufficient for you, for my power is made perfect in weakness.' Therefore I will boast all the more gladly about my weaknesses, so that Christ's power may rest on me." (2 Cor. 12:9)

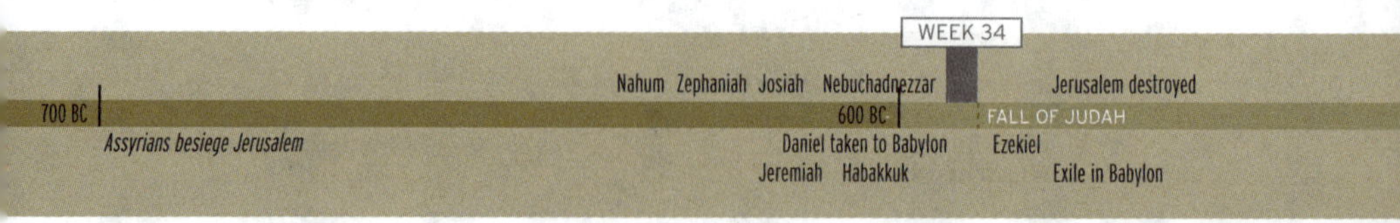

The promised Messiah

Jeremiah 33:14–18

14"'The days are coming,' declares
the Lord, 'when I will fulfil the
gracious promise I made to the
house of Israel and to the house
of Judah.
15In those days and at that time
I will make a righteous Branch
sprout from David's line;
he will do what is just and right
in the land.
16In those days Judah will be saved
and Jerusalem will live in safety.
This is the name by which it will
be called:
The Lord Our Righteousness.'
17For this is what the Lord says:
'David will never fail to have a man
to sit on the throne of the house
of Israel, 18nor will the priests, who
are Levites, ever fail to have a
man to stand before me continually
to offer burnt offerings, to burn
grain offerings and to present
sacrifices.'"

Jeremiah buys a field
Jeremiah 32:6–15

Jeremiah's prayer
Jeremiah 32:16–25

The Lord's answer
Jeremiah 32:26–35

The Lord's promise
Jeremiah 32:36–44

The restoration of the Jews
Jeremiah 33:1–13

The promised Messiah
Jeremiah 33:14–26

A message for Zedekiah
Jeremiah 34:1–7

Jeremiah in the well
Jeremiah 38:1–13

For Thought and **Contemplation**

Has life's circumstances cast you, like Jeremiah, into a well? Figuratively, we mean. Well, look up, for we are told that even in the daytime one can see the stars shining from the bottom of a well. And what do they say? "God's in His heaven – all's right with the world."

"Consider it pure joy, my brothers, whenever you face trials of many kinds, because you know that the testing of your faith develops perseverance. Perseverance must finish its work so that you may be mature and complete, not lacking anything." (Jas. 1:2–4)

Zerubbabel and main party return | *Iron Age begins in Britain* | Ezra returns | Malachi

500 BC | 400 BC

Cyrus | Zechariah Haggai | 2nd Temple built | Nehemiah rebuilds walls of Jerusalem

The fall of Jerusalem

Zedekiah seeks advice
Jeremiah 38:14–27

Message to Ebed-Melech
Jeremiah 39:15–18

The fall of Jerusalem
Jeremiah 38:28

The famine
2 Kings 25:3, Jeremiah 52:6

Fall of Judah 586 BC

The Babylonian princes
Jeremiah 39:2–3

Zedekiah's flight and capture
2 Kings 25:4–5, Jeremiah 39:4–5, 52:7–8

The slaughter
2 Chronicles 36:17

Zedekiah's sons slain
Jeremiah 52:9–10, 39:6

His blindness
Ezekiel 12:13–14, 2 Kings 25:6–7,
Jeremiah 39:7, 52:11

Temple and walls destroyed
2 Kings 25:8–10, 2 Chronicles 36:19,
Jeremiah 39:8, 52:12–14

Jeremiah 39:15–18

**15While Jeremiah had been
confined in the courtyard of the
guard, the word of the Lord came
to him: 16"Go and tell Ebed-Melech
the Cushite, 'This is what the Lord
Almighty, the God of Israel, says:
I am about to fulfil my words
against this city through disaster,
not prosperity. At that time they
will be fulfilled before your eyes.
17But I will rescue you on that day,
declares the Lord; you will not be
handed over to those you fear.
18I will save you; you will not fall by
the sword but will escape with
your life, because you trust in me,
declares the Lord.'"**

For Thought and **Contemplation**

Sad though the fall of Jerusalem was, it is important to remember that from God's point of view, those walls were ever upright before Him (Isa. 49:16). God sees with a double vision. He sees things, not only as they are, but as they will be. Our hope must be His hope.

"Remember the former things, those of long ago; I am God, and there is no other; I am God, and there is none like me. I make known the end from the beginning, from ancient times, what is still to come. I say: My purpose will stand, and I will do all that I please." (Isa. 46:9–10)

a bird's eye view of **Lamentations**

Place in the Bible

Twenty-fifth Old Testament book; third book of prophecy.

Special features

Laments.

The fifth and sixth deportations

DAY **235**

Psalm 94:1–7

[1]O Lord, the God who avenges,
O God who avenges, shine forth.
[2]Rise up, O Judge of the earth;
pay back to the proud what they deserve.
[3]How long will the wicked, O Lord,
how long will the wicked be jubilant?
[4]They pour out arrogant words;
all the evildoers are full of boasting.
[5]They crush your people, O Lord;
they oppress your inheritance.
[6]They slay the widow and the alien;
they murder the fatherless.
[7]They say, "The Lord does not see;
the God of Jacob pays no heed." ...

Fifth deportation: the poor left behind
2 Kings 25:11–12, 2 Chronicles 36:20–21, Jeremiah 39:9–10, 52:15–16

God the judge of all
Psalm 94:1–23

The Temple looted
2 Kings 25:13–17, 2 Chronicles 36:18, Jeremiah 52:17–23

Priests deported
2 Kings 25:18, Jeremiah 52:24

Prayer for nation's deliverance
Psalm 74:1–23, 79:1–13

Important men killed
2 Kings 25:19–21, Jeremiah 52:25–27

For Thought and **Contemplation**

In the midst of desolation and catastrophe, where can one turn? Thankfully, those who know the Lord can lean hard upon His breast (Psalm 74). The old adage, though a cliché, is still reassuring: when the outlook is dark and depressing, try the uplook!

"God is our refuge and strength, an ever-present help in trouble. Therefore we will not fear, though the earth give way and the mountains fall into the heart of the sea ..." (Psa. 46:1–2)

Jesus and the Book

The opening poem of Lamentations depicts Jerusalem mourning over the destruction of its city and its temple. Jesus also wept over Jerusalem, reflecting His heartfelt love for the rebellious people of Jerusalem (Matt. 23:37–38).

Teaching

For the Jews the capture of Jerusalem in 586 BC was the ultimate disaster. They no longer had their land, their city or their temple. It was as if they no longer had God! But there is a shaft of light in chapter 3:22–24.

A Verse to Remember

"Because of the Lord's great love we are not consumed, for his compassions never fail. They are new every morning; great is your faithfulness" (Lam. 3:22–23).

DAY **236** Jeremiah laments Jerusalem's fate

Jerusalem's miserable state
Lamentations 1:1–11

Jerusalem's sorrow
Lamentations 1:12–22

The Lord's terrible punishment
Lamentations 2:1–10

Jeremiah's deep sorrow
Lamentations 2:11–22

His suffering
Lamentations 3:1–20

His hope
Lamentations 3:21–30

The Lord's mercy
Lamentations 3:31–36

Lamentations 3:31–36

31 For men are not cast off
by the Lord for ever.
32 Though he brings grief, he will show compassion,
so great is his unfailing love.
33 For he does not willingly bring affliction
or grief to the children of men.
34 To crush underfoot
all prisoners in the land,
35 to deny a man his rights
before the Most High,
36 to deprive a man of justice –
would not the Lord see such things?

For Thought and **Contemplation**

The more Jeremiah looked at the troubles of Israel, the more he was grieved. The more he looked on God's mercy, however, the more his spirit revived. It's not wrong to look at your difficulties and your problems, but it is wrong to look *only* at them. Do as one great saint said: "I glance at my difficulties, but I *gaze* at God."

"What, then, shall we say in response to this? If God is for us, who can be against us?" (Rom. 8:31)

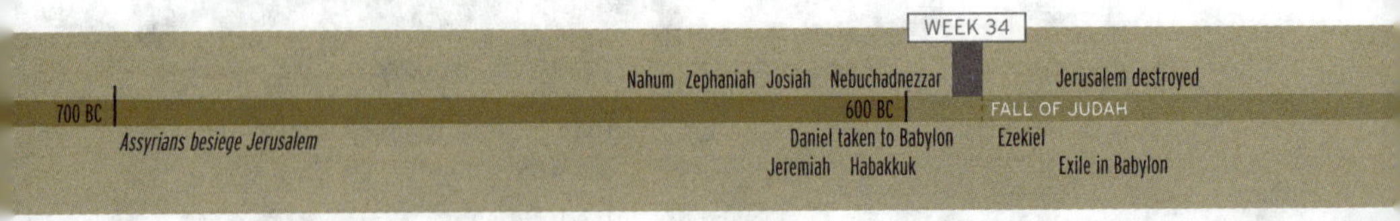

Unexpected kindness

DAY **237**

Jeremiah 40:1–4

[1]The word came to Jeremiah from the Lord after Nebuzaradan commander of the imperial guard had released him at Ramah. He had found Jeremiah bound in chains among all the captives from Jerusalem and Judah who were being carried into exile to Babylon. [2]When the commander of the guard found Jeremiah, he said to him, "The Lord your God decreed this disaster for this place. [3]And now the Lord has brought it about; he has done just as he said he would. All this happened because you people sinned against the Lord and did not obey him. [4]But today I am freeing you from the chains on your wrists. Come with me to Babylon, if you like, and I will look after you; but if you do not want to, then don't come. Look, the whole country lies before you; go wherever you please."

Jeremiah's plea
Lamentations 3:37–66

Jerusalem after the fall
Lamentations 4:1–22

A prayer for mercy
Lamentations 5:1–22

Gedaliah becomes governor
2 Kings 25:22–24

Kindness shown to Jeremiah
Jeremiah 39:11–13

Jeremiah stays with Gedaliah
Jeremiah 39:14, 40:1–5

The captivity 586–516 BC

Gedaliah's care for the poor
Jeremiah 40:6–12

For Thought and **Contemplation**

When Jeremiah was in need of help he found it, not through his own people, but through Nebuzaradan, one of the oppressors of his people. It's a sad and sobering thought, that often God's people meet with more kindness from unbelievers than they do from their Christian brothers and sisters. Ought not this to be a matter of great prayer and concern?

"Carry each other's burdens, and in this way you will fulfil the law of Christ." (Gal. 6:2)

Zerubbabel and main party return | 500 BC | *Iron Age begins in Britain* | Ezra returns | Malachi | 400 BC
Cyrus | Zechariah Haggai | 2nd Temple built | Nehemiah rebuilds walls of Jerusalem

No help in Egypt

Gedaliah killed
Jeremiah 40:13–16, 41:1–9, 2 Kings 25:25

Ishmael's escape
Jeremiah 41:10–15

The exodus to Egypt
2 Kings 25:26, Jeremiah 41:16–18

Jeremiah's assistance requested
Jeremiah 42:1–6

Safety in Judah
Jeremiah 42:7–12

Destruction in Egypt
Jeremiah 42:13–22

Jeremiah taken to Egypt
Jeremiah 43:1–7

Conquest of Egypt foretold
Jeremiah 43:8–13

Jeremiah 42:1–6

**1 Then all the army officers,
including Johanan son of Kareah
and Jezaniah son of Hoshaiah, and
all the people from the least to the
greatest approached 2 Jeremiah
the prophet and said to him,
"Please hear our petition and pray
to the Lord your God for this entire
remnant. For as you now see,
though we were once many, now
only a few are left. 3 Pray that the
Lord your God will tell us where
we should go and what we
should do."
4 "I have heard you," replied
Jeremiah the prophet. "I will
certainly pray to the Lord your
God as you have requested; I will
tell you everything the Lord says
and will keep nothing back
from you."
5 Then they said to Jeremiah,
"May the Lord be a true and faithful
witness against us if we do not act
in accordance with everything the
Lord your God sends you to tell
us. 6 Whether it is favourable or
unfavourable, we will obey the
Lord our God, to whom we are
sending you, so that it will go well
with us, for we will obey the
Lord our God."**

For Thought and **Contemplation**

Jeremiah's message could be summed up in these words: "Don't flee to Egypt. Stand your ground against the Babylonians, face them with the truth and you will be spared." Are you running from something at this moment? Then Stop. Face your problem in God's strength. Jer. 42:11 is God's special word to you today.

"He gives strength to the weary and increases the power of the weak. Even youths grow tired and weary, and young men stumble and fall; but those who hope in the Lord will renew their strength. They will soar on wings like eagles; they will run and not grow weary, they will walk and not be faint." (Isa. 40:29–31)

WEEK 35

700 BC | *Assyrians besiege Jerusalem* | Nahum Zephaniah Josiah Nebuchadnezzar | 600 BC | Daniel taken to Babylon | Jeremiah Habakkuk | Jerusalem destroyed | FALL OF JUDAH | Ezekiel | Exile in Babylon

The Jews in Egypt

DAY **239**

Jeremiah 46:27–28

27"Do not fear, O Jacob my servant;
do not be dismayed, O Israel.
I will surely save you out of a distant place,
your descendants from the land of their exile.
Jacob will again have peace and security,
and no-one will make him afraid.
28Do not fear, O Jacob my servant,
for I am with you," declares the Lord.
"Though I completely destroy all the nations
among which I scatter you,
I will not completely destroy you.
I will discipline you but only with justice;
I will not let you go entirely unpunished."

The coming of Nebuchadnezzar
Jeremiah 46:13

The Lord's message to Jeremiah
Jeremiah 46:14–18

Egypt's overthrow
Jeremiah 46:19–26

God's promise to the Jews
Jeremiah 46:27–28

Their idolatry in Egypt
Jeremiah 44:1–14

Their refusal to reform
Jeremiah 44:15–19

Jeremiah's denouncement
Jeremiah 44:20–30

Ezekiel hears of Jerusalem's fall
Ezekiel 33:21–33

For Thought and **Contemplation**

Israel was plagued with "rabbititis". It is a condition that affects many people and makes them believe that there is no problem so big or complicated that it can't be run away from. We learned yesterday that running away from problems never solves them. Look again at Jer. 44:1–14 and you'll see why.

No temptation has seized you except what is common to man. And God is faithful; he will not let you be tempted beyond what you can bear. But when you are tempted, he will also provide a way out so that you can stand up under it." (1 Cor. 10:13)

Zerubbabel and main party return | *Iron Age begins in Britain* | Ezra returns | Malachi

500 BC | 400 BC

Cyrus | Zechariah Haggai | 2nd Temple built | Nehemiah rebuilds walls of Jerusalem

DAY **240** The seventh deportation: 582 BC

Prophecy against Ammon
Ezekiel 25:1–7

Prophecy against Moab
Ezekiel 25:8–11

Prophecy against Edom
Ezekiel 25:12–14

Prophecy against Philistia
Ezekiel 25:15–17

Prophecy against Sidon
Ezekiel 28:20–23

Blessing for Israel
Ezekiel 28:24–26

The fall of Egypt
Ezekiel 32:1–16

The world of the dead
Ezekiel 32:17–32

745 more captives taken
Jeremiah 52:30

Nebuchadnezzar's golden image
Daniel 3:1–7

Ezekiel 28:24–26

[24]"'No longer will the people of
Israel have malicious neighbours
who are painful briers and sharp
thorns. Then they will know that
I am the Sovereign Lord.
[25]This is what the Sovereign Lord
says: When I gather the
people of Israel from the nations
where they have been scattered,
I will show myself holy among
them in the sight of the nations.
Then they will live in their own
land, which I gave to my servant
Jacob. [26]They will live there in
safety and will build houses and
plant vineyards; they will live in
safety when I inflict punishment on
all their neighbours who maligned
them. Then they will know that
I am the Lord their God.'"

For Thought and **Contemplation**

Have you noticed how, in every setting of human failure, God breaks through with a heartening promise? But what is more to the point, have you learned to look for God's promises in the midst of your own failures and circumstances? They're always there – just keep on looking.

"Through these he has given us his very great and precious promises, so that through them you may participate in the divine nature and escape the corruption in the world caused by evil desires." (2 Pet. 1:4)

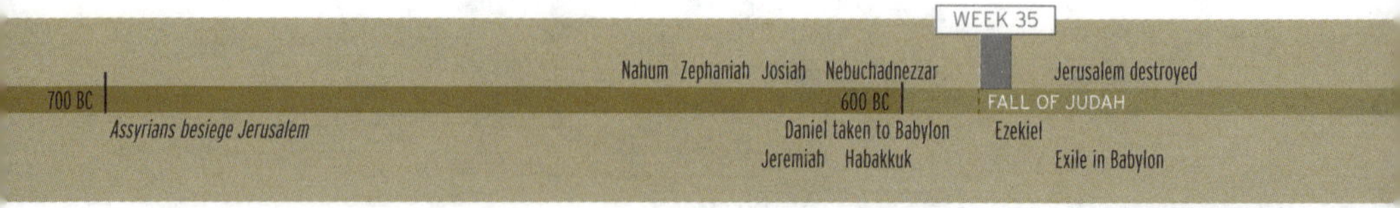

The fiery furnace

Ezekiel 34:11–16

11“‘For this is what the Sovereign
Lord says: I myself will search for
my sheep and look after them.
12As a shepherd looks after his
scattered flock when he is with
them, so will I look after my sheep.
I will rescue them from all the
places where they were scattered
on a day of clouds and darkness.
13I will bring them out from the
nations and gather them from the
countries, and I will bring them into
their own land. I will pasture them
on the mountains of Israel, in the
ravines and in all the settlements
in the land. 14I will tend them in a
good pasture, and the mountain
heights of Israel will be their
grazing land. There they will lie
down in good grazing land, and
there they will feed in a rich
pasture on the mountains of Israel.
15I myself will tend my sheep and
have them lie down, declares the
Sovereign Lord. 16I will search for
the lost and bring back the strays.
I will bind up the injured and
strengthen the weak, but the sleek
and the strong I will destroy. I will
shepherd the flock with justice.’ ”

Shadrach, Meshach and Abednego
Daniel 3:8–18

The fiery furnace
Daniel 3:19–25

Nebuchadnezzar acknowledges God
Daniel 3:26–30

His proclamation
Daniel 4:1–3

The watchman
Ezekiel 33:1–9

Individual responsibility
Ezekiel 33:10–20

Message to faithless shepherds
Ezekiel 34:1–10

The Good Shepherd
Ezekiel 34:11–16

The flock judged
Ezekiel 34:17–19

For Thought and **Contemplation**

The faith of Daniel and his friends was of a special quality. It has been called “the ‘if not’ faith”. They said: “Our God is able to deliver us ... BUT IF NOT ... we will still refuse to bow.” They believed in the rightness of their stand, irrespective of whether God delivered them or not. Ask God to give you that kind of faith. There is nothing higher.

“Now faith is being sure of what we hope for and certain of what we do not see.” (Heb. 11:1)

Zerubbabel and main party return | *Iron Age begins in Britain* | Ezra returns | Malachi

500 BC | 400 BC

Cyrus | Zechariah Haggai | 2nd Temple built | Nehemiah rebuilds walls of Jerusalem

The Bad and the Good Shepherd

The many false shepherds in Ezekiel

They fed themselves instead of the flock (34:2,3)

They had not taken care of the weak, tended the sick, bound up the broken bones, nor sought the lost (34:4)

The sheep were then scattered, having no shepherd (34:5)

Therefore, the shepherds would be punished (34:10)

They would be removed from their position as shepherds (34:10)

They would not themselves be fed by the Great Shepherd (34:10)

The Good Shepherd in Ezekiel

He would search out the lost sheep (34:11)

He would deliver them from their enemies (34:12)

He would gather them from all nations (34:13)

He would feed them upon the mountains of Israel (34:14)

He would give them rest in green pastures (34:15)

He would put splints and bandages upon their broken limbs (34:16)

He would heal the sick (34:16)

He would make an eternal pact with them (34:25)

He would guarantee their safety and place them in a perfect paradise (34:25-28)

New life

DAY **242**

Ezekiel 37:1–6

1The hand of the Lord was upon
me, and he brought me out by the
Spirit of the Lord and set me in the
middle of a valley; it was full of
bones. 2He led me to and fro
among them, and I saw a great
many bones on the floor of the
valley, bones that were very dry.
3He asked me, "Son of man, can
these bones live?"
I said, "O Sovereign Lord, you
alone know."
4Then he said to me, "Prophesy to
these bones and say to them, 'Dry
bones, hear the word of the Lord!
5This is what the Sovereign Lord
says to these bones: I will make
breath enter you, and you will
come to life. 6I will attach tendons
to you and make flesh come upon
you and cover you with skin; I will
put breath in you, and you will
come to life. Then you will know
that I am the Lord.'"

The Lord's flock
Ezekiel 34:20–31

Prophecy against Edom
Ezekiel 35:1–15

God's blessing on Israel
Ezekiel 36:1–15

Israel's former sins
Ezekiel 36:16–23

Israel's new life
Ezekiel 36:24–32

A witness to neighbouring nations
Ezekiel 36:33–38

The valley of dry bones
Ezekiel 37:1–14

For Thought and **Contemplation**

When God's people are in right standing before the Lord, the blessings that flow from this are innumerable. Some of them can be seen in Ezek. 36:24–31. How many can you find? There are at least ten.

"The blessing of the Lord brings wealth, and he adds no trouble to it." (Prov. 10:22)

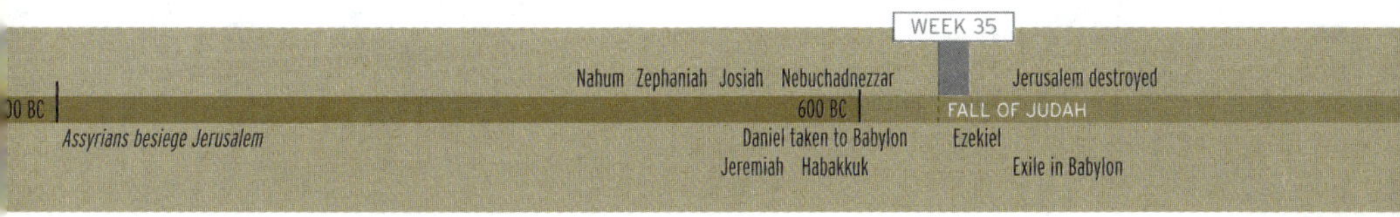

The destruction of Gog

The sign of the two sticks
Ezekiel 37:15–19

Judah and Israel to be one nation
Ezekiel 37:20–28

The malice of Gog
Ezekiel 38:1–13

God's punishment of Gog
Ezekiel 38:14–23

The defeat of Gog
Ezekiel 39:1–10

The burial of Gog
Ezekiel 39:11–20

Israel's restoration
Ezekiel 39:21–29

Ezekiel 37:24–28

**24"'My servant David will be king
over them, and they will all have
one shepherd. They will follow my
laws and be careful to keep my
decrees. 25They will live in the land
I gave to my servant Jacob, the
land where your fathers lived.
They and their children and their
children's children will live there
for ever, and David my servant will
be their prince for ever. 26I will
make a covenant of peace with
them; it will be an everlasting
covenant. I will establish them and
increase their numbers, and I will
put my sanctuary among them
for ever. 27My dwelling-place will
be with them; I will be their God,
and they will be my people. 28Then
the nations will know that I the
Lord make Israel holy, when my
sanctuary is among them for ever.'"**

For Thought and **Contemplation**

Many believe that the restoring of the nation of Israel, as predicted by Ezekiel, is taking place right before our eyes. What will happen next? Keep your finger on Ezekiel 38. This chapter may bear more relation to the events of this generation than we think.

"Pray for the peace of Jerusalem: 'May those who love you be secure. May there be peace within your walls and security within your citadels.'" (Psa. 122:6–7)

WEEK 35

Nahum Zephaniah Josiah Nebuchadnezzar Jerusalem destroyed

700 BC 600 BC FALL OF JUDAH

Assyrians besiege Jerusalem Daniel taken to Babylon Ezekiel

Jeremiah Habakkuk Exile in Babylon

Vision of future Temple

Ezekiel 40:1–4

1In the twenty-fifth year of our
exile, at the beginning of the year,
on the tenth of the month, in the
fourteenth year after the fall of the
city - on that very day the hand of
the Lord was upon me and he
took me there. 2In visions of God
he took me to the land of Israel
and set me on a very high moun-
tain, on whose south side were
some buildings that looked like a
city. 3He took me there, and I saw
a man whose appearance was like
bronze; he was standing in the
gateway with a linen cord and a
measuring rod in his hand. 4The
man said to me, "Son of man, look
with your eyes and hear with your
ears and pay attention to every-
thing I am going to show you, for
that is why you have been brought
here. Tell the house of Israel
everything you see."

Ezekiel's vision
Ezekiel 40:1–4

The East Gate
Ezekiel 40:5–16

The Outer Courtyard
Ezekiel 40:17–19

The North and South Gates
Ezekiel 40:20–27

The Inner Courtyard
Ezekiel 40:28–37

Buildings near the North Gate
Ezekiel 40:38–47

The Temple Porch
Ezekiel 40:48–49

The Most Holy Place
Ezekiel 41:1–4

The rooms
Ezekiel 41:5–12

The total measurements and details of the Temple building
Ezekiel 41:13–26

For Thought and **Contemplation**

The attention to detail which God displays in relation to His mighty works is just as evident, if you could but see it, in His personal plan for your life. Remember that the next time you are tempted to think that God might not be interested in the "little" things that go on in your life.

"Are not two sparrows sold for a penny? Yet not one of them will fall to the ground apart from the will of your Father. And even the very hairs of your head are all numbered. So don't be afraid; you are worth more than many sparrows." (Matt. 10:29-31)

Zerubbabel and main party return | *Iron Age begins in Britain* | Ezra returns | Malachi

500 BC — 400 BC

Cyrus | Zechariah Haggai | 2nd Temple built | Nehemiah rebuilds walls of Jerusalem

Heart to Heart

Section 8

Marathon runners talk of hitting the wall when they feel too exhausted to complete the course but often another competitor will encourage them to keep going. You have done so well to reach this far but if you are feeling exhausted seek encouraging prayer from a friend that you may be a faithful servant finishing what you have started.